Thinking it through

Getting answers to
life's biggest issues

MARTIN SALTER

Copyright © 2016 by Martin Salter

First published in Great Britain in 2016

The right of Martin Salter to be identified as the Author of this Work has been asserted by him in accordance with the Copyright, Designs and Patents Act 1988.

British Library Cataloguing in Publication Data

A record for this book is available from the British Library

ISBN: 978-1-910587-97-3

Designed by Mike Thorpe: www.design-chapel.com

Printed in Denmark by Nørhaven

10Publishing, a division of 10ofthose.com

Unit C, Tomlinson Road, Leyland, PR25 2DY, England

Email: info@10ofthose.com

Website: www.10ofthose.com

FOR JIM, MARK AND PHIL

(THE UNIT)

'THE UNEXAMINED LIFE IS NOT WORTH LIVING.'

Socrates

CONTENTS

ACKNOWLEDGEMENTS

Many people have been of great help in preparing this little book. Jon Putt, James Midwinter, Jim Murkett, and Thom Atkinson all offered helpful thoughts and insights, many of which served to shape the final draft. Jonathan, Felicity, and Lois from 10ofthose also contributed helpfully to the various drafts of the book. Colleagues and family members, as always, have been a source of encouragement and patience, and the editorial team at 10ofthose have been a pleasure to work with. Ultimately, if there's anything worth remembering in this book, it was a gift of God in enabling me a moment of clarity or illumination. The good bits are thanks to him; the bad bits are all mine.

Soli Deo Gloria.

INTRODUCTION

It was a bright autumnal afternoon. Golden sunlight poured in through large windows. The warmth of the sun on my neck was pleasant. The heat of the questions I was receiving was less so. Also in the room were a group of bright minds wrestling with difficult questions. They wanted to know:

- 'Why would God create people to damn them?'

- 'Where does evil come from?'

- 'What about other religions?'

- 'What about those who never hear about the Bible?'

- 'Why would God let babies die?'

- 'If murder is wrong, why does God commit mass murder in the Old Testament?'

- 'How do you reconcile a God of love with the idea of hell?'

- 'Does God hate gay people?'

These are undeniably difficult questions. But the absence of easy answers is not the same as the absence of any answers. Furthermore, these aren't just questions for 'religious' people. They are questions for *all* people. We all want to know how to make sense of famine, Ebola, genocide and human trafficking. How should we think about crime and punishment? Is there life after death? What are we to make of the plurality of religions?

This book will not attempt to answer all of these questions, nor will it offer simple answers. It will attempt something altogether more basic and, at the same time, altogether more difficult. What we need is to be taught is not always *what* to think, but *how* to think. What we need is a mental map for navigating difficult questions.

WHAT WE NEED IS A MENTAL MAP.

As one writer has noted, in our culture we are more likely to have an exchange of feelings when we disagree with someone rather than a serious attempt to *think* through issues.[1] Romanticism and postmodernism have made us emotionally richer but intellectually poorer. What we need is to regain a framework for thinking through difficult issues. To be clear, I am not suggesting that feelings are unimportant or irrelevant. And I'm not suggesting that we should be intellectual bulldozers riding roughshod over others' opinions. What I am saying is that to truly love people we need to help one another think clearly through the issues that tug most at our heart strings.

I'm increasingly convinced that many students, from primary school onwards, are taught what to think, but not how to think. They're bombarded all the time with various 'authorities'. Their pronouncements come at such a pace there is little time to reflect, analyse, and respond to them. Nor does this apply to just children and teens. Our instant information culture means that our moral imagination is formed at breakneck speed, usually on the basis of what others tell us to think or feel. We all too easily follow the crowd without ever questioning whether we've taken a wrong turn somewhere along the way.

Don't believe me? Consider this. If we'd lived in the southern states of America in the eighteenth century could we honestly say we would have seen slavery as wrong?[2] If we'd lived 200 years ago would we have had a problem with women not being able to vote? You'd have been in the minority if so. A hundred and fifty years ago we wouldn't have thought twice about child labour and working conditions. If we were raised in Germany in the early part of the 21st-century we would have viewed the First World War as a holy war, with God on our side – *'Gott mit uns'* would have been our slogan.[3] If you're raised in 21st-century Britain it seems obvious to most that abortion or gay marriage are inalienable rights; that wouldn't have been the case fifty years ago. We are inevitably products of our culture, and our values are caught from, or taught by, those we look up to and respect. So, for the sake of clarity, I'll repeat my aim: I don't so much want to tell you *what* to think as to open up a discussion on *how* to think.

In chapter one we'll explore some good questions to ask when analysing arguments. In chapter two we'll explore some of the different 'authorities' we appeal to and the ways in which they are both helpful and yet limited. In chapter three we'll think about the various ways in which arguments can go bad. In chapter four we'll explore a way forward in terms of a reliable authority source to which we can appeal in our moral reasoning. Finally, in chapter five, we'll attempt to work through some examples. These examples will not be explored in exhaustive detail. Rather we'll use the tools and framework developed in chapters one to four to begin the exploration of difficult issues.

All of us believe what seems reasonable to us. In that sense we are all 'logicians' (thinkers!). What we are attempting here is to do consciously that which we have done semi-consciously since we were about four.[4] As Bowell and Kemp note, 'Critical thinking enables us to ensure that we have good reasons to believe or do that which people attempt to persuade us to do or to believe.'[5] So, with that in mind, let's do some thinking about thinking.[6]

1

SIX HONEST SERVING-MEN

ASKING THE RIGHT QUESTIONS

Independent critical thinking is something of a lost art today. One consequence of a digital age is that we're bombarded with information all the time. 'Headspace' – that is the space to pause, ponder, think, and reflect – is at a premium, and often crowded out by the next blog post, podcast, YouTube video, link from Facebook, Twitter update, or trawl through Instagram or Pinterest. My browser has many of these running all the time, and I'm easily distracted by the newest notification or post. And sadly, all too often, it can lead to lazy, uncritical engagement. While this instant access to so much information is a wonderful gift, it can mean that people form their views at breakneck speed based on the latest social media trends. For example, Facebook invites me to cover my profile picture with a rainbow flag in support of the American Supreme Court's landmark decision to legalise same-sex marriage. Everyone else is doing it; one click and I'm done! Wait a minute; what am I agreeing to exactly?

Time to read and reflect is now seen as an unaffordable luxury. As a consequence people who hold differing opinions are often viewed with suspicion or derision. Dismissal (or even rage) has replaced serious, careful, charitable engagement.[1] And our greatest fear is that someone might be offended by our opinion.[2] It's hard to swim against the current. We may disagree with those on the extremes, but we need a better response than 'Everybody thinks that ... [*you fill in the blank*]'

IT'S HARD
TO SWIM
AGAINST THE
CURRENT.

John Dewey is regarded by many philosophers as the 'father' of modern thought when it comes to critical thinking.[3] Dewey defined critical thinking as follows: 'Active, persistent, and careful consideration of a belief or supposed form of knowledge in the light of the grounds which support it and the further conclusions to which it tends.'[4] Note some of the elements here: active as opposed to passive; persistent as opposed to lazy; careful as opposed to careless; and grounded as opposed to baseless. Dewey's definition is a helpful starting point for exploring how we can think actively, persistently, carefully, and reflectively.

So I'd like to introduce you to a little tool that may help us to develop a framework for thinking through difficult questions. Rudyard Kipling once wrote a poem entitled 'Six Honest Serving-Men'. It goes like this:

I KEEP six honest serving-men
　　　(They taught me all I knew);
Their names are What and Why and When
　　　And How and Where and Who.
I send them over land and sea,
　　　I send them east and west;
But after they have worked for me,
　　　I give them all a rest.
I let them rest from nine till five,
　　　For I am busy then,
As well as breakfast, lunch, and tea,
　　　For they are hungry men.
But different folk have different views;
　　　I know a person small–
She keeps ten million serving-men,
　　　Who get no rest at all!
She sends 'em abroad on her own affairs,
　　　From the second she opens her eyes –
One million Hows, two million Wheres,
And seven million Whys!

It is said that Kipling wrote the poem about his young daughter. She is the one with 10 million serving-men who get no rest at all – 'one million Hows, two million Wheres, and seven million Whys!' Those of us with kids can easily appreciate the sentiment!

However, Kipling's 'Six Honest Serving-Men' is of real value too in helping us process big questions. It just takes time, careful thought, and a bit of practice. The big questions (slightly reordered) are as follows:

1. **Who** is the authority on the question?

2. **Why** are they the best person to speak to the question?

3. **How** do they come to their conclusions on the question?

4. **What** exactly is the question for consideration?

5. **Where,** geographically and culturally, is the question being discussed?

6. **When,** historically, are we thinking about the question?

Let's consider these questions as our guides on a journey, helping us to see the issues and think through them more clearly. Here's a little diagram which may act as an aide-memoire. We'll take each question in turn, and consider how it is relevant to our thinking.

1 WHO?

That's the first important question. *Who*, exactly, gets to speak into a difficult question or issue? This first honest serving-man is so important to our reasoning that we'll return to him in the next chapter to give him some more time and thought. For now we need to note that there are, generally speaking, six main contenders:

1. Tradition (forebears)

2. Reason (experts)

3. Intuition (ourselves)

4. Book (an authoritative text, religious or otherwise)[5]

5. Experience (ourselves and others)

6. Society at large (majority view)[6]

On any issue we'll have to decide who gets to be the voice (or voices) of authority. Most of us will listen to multiple perspectives before coming to our own conclusion. The issue may be relatively insignificant, such as whether those trousers go with those shoes. You might ask your mum, your friends, or *Marie Claire*, but ultimately I guess you'll come to your own conclusion. On the other hand, it might be something massive – like the decision to invade another country. Who speaks then? Well, we tend to leave that to those in positions of power, and we trust that they go through a thorough process before taking such a decision (though we may protest against that conclusion). You'd hope that they seek out some experts for advice; you'd hope they might listen to history; you'd hope they talk it through with colleagues; and then you'd hope they make the right decision for the right reasons. On other issues, let's say whether Britain should remain part of the European Union, you might have a referendum. In that case the nation speaks, or at least those who bother to turn out to vote speak.

WHO SPEAKS THEN?

What about laws concerning assisted dying? Again, different perspectives will be heard – from medical experts to those who have gone through difficult end-of-life situations. Often popular celebrities have a significant voice in campaigning for a particular position. Politicians will gauge a sense of their own constituency's mind, and after much debate the government will process some legislation, one way or the other (or kick it into the long grass).

At this stage we are not yet evaluating the rights or wrongs; we're simply acknowledging that for every issue we have to consider *who* it is that gets to speak into it. Whose voice is authoritative? As I said, this issue is important enough to warrant some more attention in the next chapter. But this raises our next important question: *why* them?

2 WHY?

It is not enough to consider *who* gets to speak to an issue – we really need to dwell on *why* them, and not others. We normally listen to one voice over others for a reason. Where debated issues are concerned there is the presumption that there is more than one point of view. So who do we listen to, and, more importantly, why do we listen to them? Our 'who' might be particularly intelligent or persuasive. They might be experienced or influential. They might have power or reputation. They may simply be the majority opinion on a subject, and it's difficult to go against the herd.

Let's think about a few examples. You may decide to exercise, diet, or cut down on smoking or drinking alcohol because your doctor tells you it would be good for your health. He shows you pictures of what's happening to your arteries and lungs, and explains the likely outcome. Since he's the expert, you choose to follow his advice. You might, however, decide that you enjoy fast food, fags, and four pints a night, and choose to ignore the doctor. In this case your desire for enjoyment trumps the doctor's expertise. It's worth noting that following expert advice only works in some situations. For example, you might not take fashion advice from your pharmacist, and presumably you wouldn't take financial advice from a plumber (unless they were also a qualified financial advisor!). Additionally, some situations aren't black and white. No expert in the world can tell you whether you should have Marmite or peanut butter on your toast in the morning. That's your call.

In other instances the 'expert' may be the person or people

who know us best. Careers advisors can take you so far, but I suspect many of us listen to the voice of parents or friends more when thinking about vocation. They know us well, and, in the case of our parents, they have valuable life experiences to share, and years of accumulated wisdom to pass on. When it comes to deciding who to date we'll often listen to the advice of friends. If they know us well, and they know the other person, we'll listen to what they have to say – their opinion matters. But often the heart leads the head in such issues. In the retail industry you'll listen to your customers – they're always right, apparently. Companies will spend tens of thousands on market research to enable them to do the right thing. In this case they are listening to customers because if they don't they might not be left with any. And sometimes we feel that we just have to follow our hearts. When the experts, friends, family, and majority opinion just can't tell you what you should do, you have to go with what you feel.

YOU HAVE TO GO WITH WHAT YOU FEEL.

As you can see, some of these authorities are weightier than others. Often the more black and white the situation, the more an expert authority can help. Where the situation is more complex we're left with a more subjective basis for determining right and wrong. Part of the challenge of sound thinking is determining which authority (or combination of authorities) is best placed to inform a particular decision. The fact is we'll all appeal to some authority; the question is whether that's a good call or not.

3 HOW?

The next question to consider is *how*, exactly, the various authorities go about the decision-making process. For the experts it's often a case of cold, hard empirical evidence. If the wisdom of family and friends is the guide, it's often done on the basis of past experiences – it's anecdotal. If it's gut instinct, well, then, it's just that. If a book is our reference point, then questions of interpretation and application are to the fore. Experience-based reasoning raises questions over selective use of such evidence – what if someone else's experience is different to mine? What if I myself have conflicting experiences? And societal views raise questions around proper representation.[7] Whatever the process or method involved, it's crucial to be aware of *how* people are thinking through issues, and on what basis they come to their conclusions. Appeal to an expert is not enough. We have to be sure that good methodology is employed by our cited authorities.

In 1998 Andrew Wakefield published research in a British medical journal, *The Lancet*, claiming a link between autism and the MMR vaccine. He announced his findings via a press conference at the Royal Free Hospital. His claims made front page news, and thousands of parents were left wondering whether to give the MMR to their children or, if they already had, what the effect may be of the vaccine on their children. The media campaign even asked then Prime Minister Tony Blair whether he'd given his infant son Leo the vaccine. After some further investigation into Wakefield's research it transpired that

WHAT IF I MYSELF HAVE CONFLICTING EXPERIENCES?

his findings were bogus. His sample size was too small, his methodology was poor, and he had a conflict of interests which caused him to manipulate his data. After a lengthy investigation the General Medical Council found Wakefield guilty of serious professional misconduct, and he was struck off the medical register in 2010.

This example shows why methodology matters. Wakefield made some serious claims that affected many people. He was a doctor and a scientist – surely he had to be taken seriously? Tragically, though, his methods and motives were wrong, and his advice should not have been heeded. The how question is thus crucial to the decision-making process. We'll return to think some more about how arguments go bad in chapter three.

4 WHAT?

The fourth honest serving-man asks the 'what' question – *what* exactly is the issue or question under consideration. These remaining questions – of 'what', 'where' and 'when' – are really about clearing the ground and working out what exactly we're talking about. We've already noticed that certain authorities are better placed to speak to some things than others. Let's consider an uncontroversial example like immigration(!). The statisticians can give us a breakdown of how many enter and leave the country each year but they aren't able to tell us if our infrastructure can support that. The economists can tell us how much immigrants contribute or take from our economy but they can't tell us about the pressure they put on public services. Uncle Jim can tell us his story of nightmare neighbours who've come into the area but then Sally down the road might tell

WHAT EXACTLY IS THE ISSUE OR QUESTION UNDER CONSIDERATION.

us how wonderful her new foreign colleagues are. The media might produce stories and documentaries about the countless Romanians flooding into the UK and about others smuggling themselves into the country on lorries or through the Eurotunnel.

We need to recognise the limits of each authority's voice in the discussion if we are to come to informed and balanced conclusions. We'll need to carefully sift multiple perspectives. And, in addition, we need to work out *what* we are talking about. Is it economics, justice, social cohesion, personal preference, or perhaps a mixture of them all? Are discussions around, say, human sexuality about justice for others or personal liberty? Are

WE'LL NEED TO CAREFULLY SIFT MULTIPLE PERSPECTIVES.

those two things necessarily opposed? What if my 'rights' impinge on somebody else's rights? What if my freedom of expression seeks to deny somebody else's? Often complex ethical questions are about so much more than the presenting issue. We need to determine what we are really talking about. Failure to properly define the question will inevitably lead to incomplete, unsophisticated, and unsatisfying answers.

5 WHERE?

WHO? WHY? HOW? WHAT? **WHERE?** WHEN?

These last two questions – 'where' and 'when' – are more important than they may at first seem. The fifth question is really this: 'Does this authority (whichever one it is) get to speak on this issue to all people everywhere?' Alternatively, is there something limiting about the sphere into which they speak?

Perhaps an example will make this clear. On 18 September 2014 Briton Ray Cole was in Morocco, stood at a bus stop, with his partner Jamal Walk Nass.[8] Moroccan police arrested the pair of them on suspicion of homosexual acts and they both received a four-month prison sentence for homosexual activity. The evidence cited was, apparently, photos on a mobile phone. Homosexuality is illegal in Morocco (as it is in other parts of the world, and used to be in the UK). The British media ran the story and the Foreign Office got involved.

A similar case occurred with President Obama's recent visit to Kenya where he was determined to deliver a 'strong message on gay rights'.[9] He said, 'If somebody is a law-abiding citizen, who is going about their business ... and not harming anybody, the idea that they are going to be treated differently or abused because of who they love is wrong. Full stop.' However, the Kenyan President, Uhuru Kenyatta, disagreed saying that there were 'some things that we must admit we don't share – our culture, our societies don't accept ... It's very difficult for us [the Kenyan government] to be able to impose on [our] people that which they themselves do not accept'.

WHO IS RIGHT AND WHO IS WRONG?

Now the real question is this: do we, the British people or government (or American people or government) get to speak to the rights or wrongs of a foreign people and their government? If so, why? If not, why not? The answer to that question is not immediately obvious. For many people there is an instinctive 'yes', but, if so, surely other governments should be able to attack us for our different views? Who is right and who is wrong? And how do you know? The 'where' question should make us stop, pause, and consider more carefully the cultural and contextual forces at work.

6 WHEN?

WHO? WHY? HOW? WHAT? WHERE? WHEN?

This last question is related to the previous one. The essence of the question is: 'Does this authority get to speak on this issue to all people throughout history?' In other words, is the authority speaking on behalf of all people in all times and places or just a people/person in a particular time and place?

Take the story of Ray Cole just cited. He would also have been considered a criminal in the UK within the last fifty years. Is that right or wrong? And why? Is our authority, in our time and place, more enlightened than another? Or are we simply representing the majority view in our time and place? Does the expert finding hold true for all times and places or may something, as yet to be discovered, contradict current opinion? The experts, at one time, thought the world was flat, and that the sun travelled around the earth. Who is to say another scientific revolution won't undermine much of what we currently take for granted? Our parents (and grandparents) held certain views about sex, sexuality, marriage, and divorce. Were they wrong? What will our grandchildren think of some of our current thinking? Will my gut instinct tomorrow contradict my gut instinct today – or are they both right in their time? These questions are actually incredibly important. It's easy to think that our culture has worked it all out. If history is anything to go by, then, in reality future generations will likely deem us fools for our views on some issues.

Questions of 'when' and 'where' open up a crucial aspect of this discussion – are right and wrong universal or relative categories? Is something always right or always wrong? Are some things right or wrong for that person in that situation? Is taking another life always wrong? What about in

IS SOMETHING ALWAYS RIGHT OR ALWAYS WRONG?

self-defence, or for a member of the armed forces? Is lying always wrong? What if you're hiding Jews in your basement and the Gestapo come knocking? To some degree these questions are answered by the 'who'. If I'm the authority in a situation, then right and wrong become relative to me in my circumstances. If the government is the authority, then right and wrong applies to all the people under their jurisdiction. If God is the authority, then right and wrong become categories that apply to all people in all times and places. These sorts of questions reveal just how complex ethical thinking really is.

KEEP ASKING QUESTIONS

The six honest serving-men – 'who', 'what', 'why', 'how', 'where', and 'when' – provide a helpful framework for beginning to define and consider complex questions. If we could boil all of this down to just two key questions they would be these: 'Who says?' and 'Where did they get that from?' On any opinion, be it political, religious, or ethical, you should always ask the 'who' question. The second question – 'Where did they get that from?' – to some degree covers the other honest serving-men addressing the 'why', 'how', 'what', 'where', and 'when'. Here's a few examples:

- Who says we were right to go to war? Where do they get that from?

- Who says that bag goes with those shoes? Where do they get that from?

- Who says all religions lead to God? Where do they get that from?

- Who says Arsenal are the best team in the league? Where do they get that from?

- Who says abortion is OK? Where do they get that from?

- Who says the country is overcrowded? Where do they get that from?

- Who says adoption by gay couples is a good thing? Where do they get that from?

And if two questions are too many for you to consider, you can go even further and become like a three-year-old again, simply demanding, 'Why? Why? Why?' It's kind of annoying, but it forces thoughtful engagement with an issue that gets us beyond the 'Everyone thinks that ...' or 'It just feels right.'

I said at the start of this chapter that the 'who' question is sufficiently important to warrant further reflection; to that we now turn.

2
TRIBES: THE COMPETING AUTHORITIES
THE VOICES WE LISTEN TO

There are a number of 'authorities' clamouring for our attention. The main contenders, as we saw in the previous chapter, are tradition, reason, intuition, a book, experience, or society at large. The eagle-eyed will notice that the initial letters of each 'authority' spells the word 'TRIBES', which may be apt since often discussion between these authorities can feel a little like tribal warfare. To be clear, and give you a sense of where we're going, I want to suggest that each of these authorities can be useful, but not ultimately determinative, in the way in which one answers life's biggest questions. Let's consider each one in turn.

The Competing Authorities

- TRADITION (FOREBEARS)
- REASON (EXPERTS)
- INTUITION (OURSELVES)
- BOOK (RELIGIOUS OR OTHERWISE)
- EXPERIENCE (OURSELVES AND OTHERS)
- SOCIETY AT LARGE (MAJORITY VIEW)

1 TRADITION (FOREBEARS)

What do our parents think and which of our values are informed by our heritage? For many of us, at least a part of the way in which we view the world and think about big questions is informed by the things we were taught by the people we trusted most – our parents. As a society our UK laws are based upon Christian heritage and tradition. Our culture places a high value on democracy, justice, and care for the needy. For many of these good things we are thankful to our parents, and their parents, and those that went before them.

But not all tradition is good. For example, in ancient Rome the Twelve Tables of Roman Law permitted fathers to sell their sons into slavery. In eighteenth-century India widow-burning was an accepted and practised custom. If we'd lived in Britain 150 years ago our tradition wouldn't have thought much about labour rights, working conditions, and the minimum wage. So if tradition can be both good and bad we need to think hard about the criteria by which we judge our traditional beliefs. We need to keep asking questions such as, 'Is the traditional view on this belief or practice right or wrong? Why?' The answer 'It just is' as a reason is pretty flimsy, and not something we should be happy to settle for.

A little while ago I visited a Korean couple in their home. They requested I took my shoes off in the porch – a custom for them, and fine by me (until I discovered I was wearing my holey socks). Besides, my wife makes me take my shoes off at home too. And then the couple sat me down on their sofa and offered me a drink and something to eat. That was also fine by me. And then they did something both unexpected and a little unnerving. They both sat down

NOT ALL
TRADITION
IS GOOD.

on the floor in front of me. I didn't say anything obviously because I'm English and we don't know how to deal with social situations we find awkward. It turns out it is just a simple way of honouring a guest in their culture and that is why they did it. Their parents taught them how to treat guests. They didn't learn it by empirical data or gut feeling. It is part of their cultural heritage and tradition.

Many of us have traditional practices handed down through generations, and some of our beliefs, values, and behaviours have travelled the same path. In our culture many people still want to get married before they start a family, and often people want to marry in a church even though they wouldn't describe themselves as particularly religious. Many of these things are part of our own cultural heritage and tradition.

For some issues this works well, but in other cases we seek to deliberately overturn tradition, as has recently been the case, for example, with the definition of marriage in the UK and many other countries in the West. Those opposed to redefining marriage often appeal to traditional values, while those in favour call for a rejection of those 'outdated' values. Appeals to tradition are difficult in deciding issues of right and wrong precisely because we cannot agree on whether various traditions are good or bad. As we're going to see, all of the 'TRIBAL' authorities have the potential to be both helpful and harmful, and are therefore, on their own, unable to address our biggest questions satisfactorily.

2. REASON (EXPERTS)

In some cases the authority we appeal to is reason – we want to know if something is reasonable, rational, logical, and sane. We might want empirical evidence for a position: have experiments been done? Is there some scientific research that can help us navigate through our thoughts regarding an issue?

Reason can work at two different levels – the empirical and the logical.[1] The empirical is concerned with evidential proof. Someone may posit that water boils at 80 degrees centigrade. However, if you do some experiments, and then some more, and then a few extra for good measure, your repeated experiment demonstrates that water boils at 100 degrees centigrade. That is a true statement based on empirical evidence.[2]

Logic works in a slightly different way. We may employ deductive or inductive reasoning. Deduction works by a number of premises that necessarily lead to a conclusion. An often used example is as follows: all men are mortal; Socrates is a man; therefore Socrates is mortal. The premises necessarily lead to the conclusion. An argument can be said to be 'valid' when the premises logically lead to the conclusion. Additionally the argument can be said to be 'sound' if the premises are actually true. Sometimes, however, the premises aren't true. Take this next example:

people with blonde hair are more intelligent than people who don't have blonde hair; Sally has blonde hair and Sue has brown hair; therefore Sally is more intelligent than Sue. Now, logically speaking, the argument is valid – the conclusion necessarily follows. However, since the premise is not true (there is no evidence to suggest people with blonde hair are more intelligent than people who don't have blonde hair) the argument is not sound. Sally *may* be more intelligent than Sue, but for a whole host of different reasons.

Logic using inductive arguments, on the other hand, work by drawing probable (but not definitive) conclusions based on observed data. For example: Tom is a taxi driver; taxi drivers are normally friendly; therefore Tom is friendly. The argument isn't quite as strong as the deductive argument, but nevertheless makes reasonable (though not infallible) conclusions based on observation. One interesting example of inductive reasoning often occurs in debate about the resurrection of Jesus

SOCRATES IS A MAN; THEREFORE SOCRATES IS MORTAL.

Christ. The reasoning often goes something like this: dead men don't rise from the dead; Jesus was dead; therefore Jesus didn't rise from the dead. But, of course, the fact that dead men don't ordinarily rise from the dead does not disprove the resurrection – it could still have happened (and there's good evidence that it did), and if it did it would truly be a world-changing event.

Reason is often pitted against the other authorities, particularly tradition or intuition. Rational thinking is not interested in how you *feel* about something; reason simply wants to know if it's true, whether it works, or if there is some hard evidence. Another good example of this is climate change. Meteorological experts analyse the data, and present the results, which in turn shape public feeling, behaviour, and policy. Of course we can't all do the scientific experiments ourselves. We put our faith and trust in the testimony of the experts. We trust that they've done their homework, that they're suitably qualified, that their methodology and presentation is sound, that they all agree, and that, fundamentally, they are right in their predictions. When we think about it like this quite a lot of faith is required from us in our experts, and, if we're to think clearly, we must entertain the possibility that they might be wrong. Repeated and independent work can increase our confidence, but the history of science encourages us that the mantra 'proceed with caution' is a good one to follow when it comes to putting all of our faith in the experts.

WE PUT OUR FAITH IN THE TESTIMONY OF THE EXPERTS.

3 INTUITION (OURSELVES)

What does our gut tell us? What just 'feels' right? It's not uncommon to watch TV talent shows and hear a judge say something along the lines of, 'I've got a feeling about you – you're going to have a big future.' More often than not they're wrong. The show finishes and the contestant fades back into obscurity.

One area of life where our hearts tend to rule our heads is love and romance. In Thomas Hardy's novel *Jude the Obscure* there is a powerful description of how Jude finds himself falling head over heels for a young lady in the village of Alfredston. All his plans and labours were directed toward attending the University at Christminster (which stands for Oxford) and pursuing ordained ministry in the Anglican Church. His passions overcome him and his head follows his heart. After it all goes sour you'd think he'd learned his lesson but nope, he does it all over again with his cousin Sue Bridehead. Young Sue is married to the middle-aged schoolmaster Phillotson, and in one powerful chapter she announces her desire to leave him for Jude, and he wrestles with what the right thing to do is. Hardy's novel is a story of hearts leading heads from start to finish.

Chip and Dan Heath wrote a book entitled *Switch* in which they explore what drives human behaviour.[3] They used the analogy of an elephant and a rider. The rider is the rational side of you – the one that makes New Year's resolutions about dieting and sets the alarm in time for work tomorrow. The elephant is the bit of you that so desires cake that the resolution is abandoned, or the bit of you that rolls over and hits 'snooze' one more time. Shops play on this dynamic all the time, being designed so as to entice your elephant aspect. Have you ever wondered why the bread and milk are at the furthest point from the door in the supermarket? It's because you have to walk past all of the lovely but naughty treats on the way, and they know your heart will probably win so you'll end up spending more money than you meant to on Gü puddings and Sensations sweet chilli crisps.

It's not just our appetite for romance or snacks that reveals the power of our desires. The intuitive sense that a kebab is the right thing for me at this moment is one thing; the intuitive sense that he or she is 'the one' is different altogether; and our 'sense' around issues of life, liberty, or justice is different again. For example, the debates surrounding end-of-life issues are often highly charged around people's feelings. Those people are not being disingenuous – they do feel strongly about their view. The problem comes when somebody feels equally strongly to

END-OF-LIFE ISSUES ARE OFTEN HIGHLY CHARGED AROUND PEOPLE'S FEELINGS.

the contrary. Who is right then? If my feelings can lead me astray with regard to late-night food or late-night flings, is it possible my feelings could mislead me on those big ethical questions too? In reality my feelings for an issue are an unreliable guide in determining whether my position is right or wrong.

4 BOOK (RELIGIOUS OR OTHERWISE)

Sometimes a person's (or group's) authority is their holy book. In determining what is right and wrong, the Bible or the Qu'ran, or the Book of Mormon, or the Bhagavad Gita may be consulted. Of course such a text requires proper interpretation. A whole host of terrible things have been done through the misunderstanding, misinterpretation, or misapplication of a holy book. Nonetheless, the text is considered authoritative by virtue of the divinity behind it. If God is the all-knowing, all-good creator then he would naturally be the voice of authority. The debate for many revolves around the evidence for the existence of such a deity and the reliability of the holy texts possessed, many of which seem to contradict each other. However, don't dismiss the religious claim too quickly – the sentiment is surely correct: *if* there is a God, who has revealed himself to man, he would be the best and only voice of authority in questions of right and wrong. The question is whether there is such a God. We'll return to this shortly.

Actually it's slightly more complicated still. While many don't profess a particular religion, many do have a spiritual belief, and even those that don't still put their faith in one of the other authorities. I've dealt with the subject in another place.[4] There is no neutrality. We all trust something – it may be modern science or philosophical reason; it may be personal intuition or experience; it may be the majority voice. Sometimes books that wouldn't be deemed 'religious' carry enduring influence. In May 2014 Jean Ferraiuolo published a list of the ten most influential books of all time.[5] The list included Plato's *The Republic*; Sun Tzu's *The Art of War*; Machiavelli's *The Prince*; Karl Marx and Frederick Engels' *The Communist Manifesto*; Adam Smith's *The Wealth of Nations*; and Charles Darwin's *The Origin of Species*. All of these texts, though not considered 'holy', have exercised significant influence as authority sources. In some ways these texts function in the same way as religious texts. They are authority sources which are appealed to in their particular spheres. And those that appeal to their authority often do so in the same faith-like way that religious people adhere to their texts. Since most of us don't have the time, ability, or expertise to investigate all the issues for ourselves, we all end up exercising some sort of faith in our various authorities. At some point we all exercise faith in our chosen authority.

5 EXPERIENCE (OURSELVES AND OTHERS)

Experience can undoubtedly be a valuable tool in attempting to address difficult questions. Bertrand Russell distinguished between knowledge *about* something and the knowledge *of* something[6]. It's one thing to know about the effects of roller coasters on the human body; it's another thing to have such knowledge first-hand. To use another example, it is one thing to understand the physics involved in riding a bike; it's another to know it through experience – it's a different sort of knowledge.[7]

Those who've lived longer than us have seen enough of life to have a sense of whether something is wise, unwise, right, or wrong. As the philosopher George Santayana said, 'Those who cannot remember the past are condemned to repeat it.'[8] It may be a simple thing – you

'THOSE WHO CANNOT REMEMBER THE PAST ARE CONDEMNED TO REPEAT IT.'

lied when you were eight, got caught for it, and so have vowed never to lie again. Your past experience shapes your current belief and practice. It may be a life-changing experience that shapes your view of a difficult issue. Lesley Bassett watched her friend Sylvia Alper slowly degenerate and suffer under the cruel effects of Multiple Sclerosis. Unable to afford the trip to Switzerland to attend

EXPERIENCE CAN BE A USEFUL GUIDE, BUT A POOR MASTER.

a euthanasic clinic, she secured the necessary drugs online, took her friend to a bedsit in Eastbourne, and helped her to end her suffering.[9] Or who can forget the incredibly emotional portrayal of the same issue in the soap opera *Coronation Street*. I can't imagine what it must be like to watch a loved one suffer a slow and painful death. It undoubtedly affects your view on the rights and wrongs of assisted dying. Of course the danger is that our experiences so colour our view that we find it difficult, if not impossible, to hear another side of the argument without feeling personally enraged. We may find it difficult to hear someone else's experience of outstanding palliative care. We may find it difficult to understand another's concern about the potential unintended consequences of legalising assisted dying. Our experience shapes us, but we need, if we're to be careful thinkers, to be able to step back from our experience to appreciate the web of related issues and arguments. Like many of these authorities we are talking about, experience can be a useful guide, but a poor master.

6 SOCIETY AT LARGE (MAJORITY VIEW)

It is difficult to overestimate the power of society at large to shape our own personal view of an issue. We've all experienced peer pressure at some stage in our lives. Well, the same thing can happen with regard to our beliefs, values, attitudes, and behaviour. The difficulty, of course, is in attempting to ascertain the relationship between individual and societal values. It's the age-old chicken versus egg conundrum. Are societal views simply a reflection of individual views or is there a way in which societal views shape individual values? At one level what 'society' thinks is simply a reflection of what is already out there.[10] That is why extreme opinions are ignored, rebuffed, or mocked. Ted Turnau, in his study of culture, says the following:

> *The influence of popular culture on us is like a conversation: it moves back and forth between reflecting and shaping the surrounding culture and people in culture. The makers of popular culture grope and probe, trying to find what will connect, and then they expand on that territory of the popular imagination. In its own unique way, popular culture both reflects the popular imagination and informs it, doing both at the same time.*[11]

Let's take smoking as an example. In the 1920s and 1930s it was a symbol of sophistication and style – it was something almost aspirational. If you wanted to buy your partner something highly fashionable, a little silver cigarette case was the gift to give. There was no doubt that society's view in that era was that smoking was cool. That view has changed enormously even in the last ten years. Science and medicine have demonstrated the damaging effects of smoking; public policy has outlawed smoking in public places like restaurants and bars. When I was a teenager, a crafty fag was dangerously cool. Today's teenagers are generally uninterested in smoking. Yet it isn't science or scare stories that affect their, and our, view of smoking today – it's the overall societal view. If our 'society' deems it unfashionable then we will trot along behind the majority view.

Speaking of fashion, there lies perhaps the most obvious example. The designers lead the way and we slavishly follow, eager to keep up with trends, or perhaps simply eager not to stand out as odd or different. Peer pressure is a powerful force, and the pressure to conform to societal views on ethical issues is immense. Going against the herd is a sure-fire way to get yourself marginalised, persecuted, or ridiculed, often for no other reason than the fact you are in the minority. Of course society as a whole may be right, but sometimes in history it has been catastrophically wrong. The fact that a view is the majority view does not necessarily make it right.

What does all of this prove? Simply that we are all far more products of our culture than we would like to admit. As Thouless has noted:

> We all of us tend to judge problems from one particular standpoint – the one determined by our conditions of life. We are inhabitants of our own particular country, with a particular religious and moral tradition, and we are inclined to forget how many of our judgements are simply relative to this single standpoint and are not absolute.[12]

This chapter has sought to explore the various authorities we listen to – they are the 'who' that we appeal to most often in our thinking and reasoning. In reality we all appeal to the whole range in differing measure for differing questions. And as I said at the start of the chapter, these authorities are all useful, but, as we've seen, cannot be ultimately determinative for us in addressing the big questions of life. None of them are infallible. So are we resigned to defeat? We'll return after the next chapter to think about a way forward; for now we need to consider the various ways in which arguments can go bad.

3

THE ALLURE OF THE SIREN VOICES

ARGUMENTS ON SHAKY GROUND

In Greek mythology the sirens were stunning creatures with beautiful voices. They would entice sailors toward them only for the sailors to end up shipwrecked on the rocks. Intellects, like boats, can be lured off course to the wrecking of arguments. Just as there are good ways to think, there are also some bad ones. Sadly the bad arguments are often uncritically accepted, and all too often win the day.

I want to introduce you to some of the common charlatans which pass themselves off as arguments.[1] These are sometimes referred to as 'logical fallacies' and there are loads of them. They can broadly be divided into two sorts – the formal and the substantive.[2] Formal fallacies concern logical flaws in an argument; the substantive concern unjustified inferences, methods, or assumptions.

An example of the formal fallacy would be:

- Premise 1: Philosophers are wise.
- Premise 2: Jon is wise.
- Conclusion: Jon must be a philosopher.

Here we can pretty quickly work out that it's possible to be wise without being a philosopher – the conclusion does not follow from the premises.

An example of a substantive fallacy would be:

- Premise: Most people think the defendant is innocent.
- Conclusion: Therefore the defendant must be innocent.
- Hidden/implied premise: Majority opinion is always right.

Here we can see that it is the hidden assumption that is the root of the problem.

Given that most popular-level fallacies are in the substantive category, the majority of the ten examples that follow would be categorised as substantive. So, here we go.

THE BAD ARGUMENTS ARE OFTEN UNCRITICALLY ACCEPTED.

1 IF YOU'RE LOSING, SHOUT LOUDER

The basic idea of this is that he who shouts loudest, longest, or angriest, or who cries first, wins. You see it everywhere from Oprah to the Houses of Parliament. It is also known as the 'Jeremy Kyle fallacy'. One wit called it the 'Chewbacca defence' – holler until your opponent backs down.[3] Heckling, jeering, shouting, and finger-wagging are all ways of trying to make your point of view carry the day. Sometimes highly charged discussion can degenerate into personal attack. And if none of that works then start to cry – only a jerk would keep coming for you after that. Game, set, and match!

I asked an MP once why they behave like baboons during Prime Minister's Question Time. Didn't he realise that we thought they all looked like silly schoolboys incapable of intelligent adult exchange? He said he thought it was an important part of debate – cheering and jeering can support your own case and put off the other. I'm not exaggerating or misrepresenting him – that was his actual response. Whether someone is right or wrong is, apparently, irrelevant – all that counts is winning! In the run-up to the last general election the Chancellor, George Osborne, suggested that the leader of the opposition,

Ed Miliband, could take a part in a Wallace and Gromit animation after he lost the upcoming election. Hilarious! And utterly irrelevant to the discussion they were having.

An interesting, and reasonably recent, example of this sort of arguing can be seen in Stephen Fry's rhetorically charged response in an interview with Gay Byrne.[4] Fry was asked what he'd say, as an atheist, if he died and found himself facing God. He responded as follows:

> Bone cancer in children? What's that all about? How dare you, how dare you create a world in which there is such misery that is not our fault ... Why should I respect a capricious, mean-minded, stupid God who creates a world that is so full of injustice and pain?

Fry picks up on an issue keenly felt by anyone with an ounce of compassion. These are real questions that people of all faiths (or none) have wrestled with through the millennia. There are no glib and easy answers to them but there are things that can be said.[5] First, the problem of evil necessitates an absolute good otherwise suffering is simply random and meaningless. Second, is it true to say that suffering in the world is nothing to do with us? Third, is it impossible that God might have some purpose through it all, just because we don't understand it?[6] The power and force of Fry's argument is in its rhetorical form, not its substance. Inflammatory examples and language cloud clear thinking, and we need to be aware of this as we address them. Thus the attention the video generated was related to the powerful way in which Fry articulates his objections, yet the argument itself is actually not very strong – it's been muted and refuted by philosophers through the generations. The audience finds itself in agreement because Stephen Fry is a good orator and his point is made with passion, but we must remember the force with which he puts his argument is not an indicator of the strength of the argument itself.

I don't suppose any of us could claim to be immune from such behaviour. Even with our own kids emotion can take over, voices get raised, and then someone storms out of the house. It's not wrong to feel strongly about something. In fact it's important we do feel strongly about our values and beliefs – it's part of what makes us human. If we believe something to be true then it is not merely an intellectual issue but a moral one. Our beliefs should touch our hearts as well as our heads. But don't forget the strength with which you hold your view is no measure of its truthfulness; you can be sincerely wrong. The strength with which you express your view only indicates how strongly you feel; it has no bearing on whether you're right or wrong. As soon as you see your emotion for what it is you should realise that it's completely irrelevant to the rightness or wrongness of the argument. If we're to engage with people in a way which is respectful we need to be careful to listen and respond in measured ways, rather than dismiss others with raised voices or strong rhetoric.

2 WHOA, SLIPPERY SURFACE AHEAD

You may sometimes hear people talk about a 'slippery slope' or 'the thin end of the wedge', by which they mean, 'If you embrace that position you will end up, sooner or later, over there.' A good contemporary example is related to video games. You might have heard the following argument: 'If you play violent video games you'll end up killing someone.' OK, it's not normally put that crassly, but that's the essence of the argument. Similarly, others claim: 'If you smoke weed when you're sixteen you'll inevitably end up dead in a crack den before you're thirty.' Another example is that when my eldest child was four he came home from school one day and announced, 'I'm going to work really hard at school otherwise when I grow up I'll have to live in a box on the street.' Of course, wanting to encourage him to work hard, we didn't bother to correct

'THE THIN END OF THE WEDGE'.

this logical fallacy. Yet we know that a person can have the finest education money can buy and may still sadly end up without work or shelter. And we also know that it's possible to leave school with three O levels (GCSEs to you and me!) and wind up as the prime minister of the UK.[7]

Now, this whole argument isn't entirely stupid. There is some correlation between what goes in and what comes

out. There are stories of people who watch too many horror movies and end up as serial killers. But, and it's a big but, there are also thousands more who don't. Smoking weed or skiving school certainly won't help you in the world of school or work. And statistics suggest that the probabilities connected with undesirable actions and undesirable outcomes are, well, undesirable. But, at a strictly logical level, cause and effect isn't always neat and tidy. An initial action does not automatically lead to the envisaged end. Of course, if there is any correlation, that should serve (at the very least) as a strong warning. Nevertheless, slippery slope arguments are, at the level of logic, fallacious.

3 HEY THERE, SCARECROW

This is also sometimes known as the 'straw man argument'. If you want to beat someone up good, make him out of straw and kick the stuffing out of him. It's easy – he can't fight back, and he's not that hard. Of course, he's also not real – you made him up. This happens metaphorically in argument. People construct the weakest version of their opponent's case and then beat the stuffing out of it. The problem is you made the opponent's case up – it's not what they actually say, think, or feel. The victory isn't real because you haven't really engaged with the full strength of the opponent's position. Sometimes it's done deliberately, but more often than not it's done because we're too lazy to really wrestle with the best of the arguments on all sides. We too easily accept an account of things based on our pre-existing bias.

John Butterworth and Geoff Thwaites, in their book *Thinking Skills*, talk about the 'principle of charity', and suggest we should assume the best and engage with the best arguments of those with whom we disagree.[8] In this regard we need to be aware of the agendas of media outlets. Different media companies will have particular interests, and some are more fair-minded than others, but we need to consider that when we engage with media representation we may not be getting all the facts. Actually we almost certainly are not. It would take too long, be too boring, and get few views or sales to bother presenting all sides of a debate. Consider scare stories about Islamic extremism, or Eastern European workers. These sell newspapers, but the idea that all Muslims are terrorists, or that Eastern European people are solely to blame for unemployment in the UK, is a lazy straw man argument.

I watched an example of this sort of straw man argument a little while ago. It was part of comedian Ricky Gervais' stand-up show *Animals*. He was mocking Christians who believe in the Genesis account of creation. While it made his audience laugh it failed to fairly represent what Christians actually think about the issue. Had he done some research he'd have discovered that in fact Christians have a range of opinions on how best to interpret and understand Genesis 1 and 2. Some view it literally, while others view it as being more symbolic, figurative, literary, or even apologetic within its ancient Near Eastern context. Of course, Ricky Gervais doesn't care about this – his aim is to make people laugh, and caricatures are often employed well by comedians to that effect. Yet we need to recognise his skit for what it is, and not fall into the

THE IDEA THAT ALL MUSLIMS ARE TERRORISTS IS A LAZY STRAW MAN ARGUMENT.

trap of thinking he's making a sane argument about origins. Casual dismissals might sound good, but we need to be prepared to think a little more carefully and challenge such tactics wherever we see them.

4 CHARACTER ASSASSINATION

A variation on this theme is to simply attack the person: 'Oh, you can't trust politician X, he fiddled his expenses.' Of course there is, as with some other fallacies, a grain of truth here. Deceit and dishonesty do raise questions about trustworthiness. And yet, at the level of logic, we need to remember that failure in one area does not mean a person is wrong in all of their views, though smear campaigns are a common way of attempting to discredit someone else's point of view.

A serious example of this sort of thing can be seen in the story of Jeffrey Wigand, a former B&W Tobacco company employee who blew the whistle on his former employers.[9] The story was later turned into the film *The Insider* starring Russell Crowe and Al Pacino. Wigand knew that the company were putting carcinogens (chemicals capable of causing cancer) into its tobacco to improve the flavour and he went public about it. In response B&W commissioned a report on Wigand entitled 'The Misconduct of Jeffrey S. Wigand Available in the Public Record'. B&W hired a team of private investigators to dig up as much dirt on Wigand as they could. Their 'report' contained numerous allegations about supposed misdemeanours that Wigand had committed, many of which were unproven. The plan was simple – discredit Wigand and the story about them would go away. It backfired. Their report was released in full to *The Wall Street Journal* and they had failed to carefully edit the good evidence from the unproven. Rather than discrediting Wigand, B&W simply served to add fuel to the fire of every conspiratorial notion surrounding big tobacco companies.[10]

Barristers employ this tactic all the time – if you can discredit the witness you can discredit their evidence. Yet while someone's character is clearly important, it is possible for them to be telling the truth with a track record of dishonesty. Logically speaking an argument is not discredited simply by discrediting the speaker. It's relatively easy for us to see through such blatant examples, but how frequently do we catch ourselves dismissing someone else's view with a simple 'Oh, well, they would say that, wouldn't they.' We've failed to engage with their argument and have simply dismissed them based upon something about their character. Character is important – don't mishear me. But at a logical level it has little bearing on the validity of an argument. Whether we like it or not it's possible for someone to be right and disliked simultaneously.

Related to this is the 'you too' (*tu quoque*) fallacy which refuses rebuttal on the basis that the opponent is guilty of the accusation.[11] An example is: 'You can't say adultery is a sin; you're on your third wife and you're only thirty-two!' However, the guilt of the proponent does not render his argument false.

5 CALL IN THE NAZIS

Another variation is guilt by association. The idea is to connect an idea to an undesirable figure or group, because then nobody will want to be in that camp. Modern satirists do this regularly with UKIP, connecting them to Hitler and the Nazi party – nobody wants to be in that camp, therefore nobody wants to vote UKIP. Of course it's a straw man – a cheap shot – and fails to engage with the very best argument that an individual, or in this case a political party, has to offer.[12]   Another example of this occurs with bankers. Five leading banks have recently been handed a hefty $5.6 billion fine for foreign exchange manipulation and Libor rigging. Following their investigation, the FBI labelled the

ANOTHER VARIATION IS GUILT BY ASSOCIATION.

banks' actions as 'criminality on a massive scale'.[13] And now 'banking' and 'bankers' have become dirty words associated with dodgy dealing and funny money. All are tarnished with the same brush, and the many suffer for the sins of the few. It's guilt by association.

Likewise, in 2007 Louis Theroux made a BBC documentary, *The Most Hated Family in America*, about the Phelps family, now infamous for their pickets in which children brandish signs with slogans such as 'God hates fags' and 'You're going to hell'. The Phelps family claim to be Christians serving God in their action, and the danger of their action

THE MANY SUFFER FOR THE SINS OF THE FEW.

(and the BBC documentary) is that all Christians can be thought to hold similar views. And seeing as nobody wants to be associated with such extreme hatred, the baby – Christianity – is thrown away with the bathwater. It's guilt by association without considering the differences in views and arguments. It's a quick and easy way of dismissing something you disagree with without having to engage with the best case of the argument. Yet, as with previous fallacies, we need to identify such guilt by association for what it is, and consider carefully the accuracy or otherwise of the claims being made.

6 IT'S BLACK OR WHITE

'Have you stopped stealing from your employer yet?'[14] How would you answer that question? 'Er, yes, I mean no, I mean I don't ... steal, that is, don't need to stop stealing ... Er ... can I start again?'

The mischief in the question is it leaves you only two options. Either you have stopped stealing from your employer, which meant you did steal at one time – not cool; or you haven't stopped stealing – even more not cool. It's an 'either-or' argument, sometimes also called the 'law of excluded middle'. Of course the right way to answer the question is to refuse the question. The question is irrelevant as it excludes the proposition that I don't steal from, nor have I ever, stolen from my employer. If the first fallacy we looked at might also be known as the 'Jeremy Kyle fallacy' we might call this one the 'Jeremy Paxman fallacy'. If you've ever watched a politician squirm in one of his *Newsnight* interviews you'll know what I mean. Paxman will often ask a question like: 'Will you continue to be utterly incompetent or will you actually introduce this piece of legislation.' Of course Paxman's question doesn't allow for the option of competence in not introducing the said piece of legislation.

Another well-known illustration of this error is given by Bertrand Russell who uses the following statement as an example: 'The present king of France is bald.' It appears to be a simple 'either-or' – it is either true or false.[15] However, the question does not allow for the possibility that there is no present king of France.

A further example was evident in David Cameron's recent comments about those who opposed the bombing in Syria; he termed them 'terrorist sympathisers'.[16] This excludes the possibility that you might be opposed to both terrorism and bombing Syria.

One final example we noted earlier was the reasoning of Stephen Fry that either God is capricious, stupid, and mean-minded, or he's not really there at all. It sounds compelling, but it fails to allow for the possibility that life might not be that simple. The fact is we like simple and straightforward – it's just easier. Yet, in reality, issues are often much more complex.

A variety of this mistake concerns generalisations. There are 'hard' generalisations and 'soft' generalisations.[17] The latter are easier to justify; the former much harder. You can spot generalisations by the use of words like 'all', 'some', 'most', and 'none'. An example of a 'hard' generalisation would be: 'All men drive too fast.' The problem with this argument is you only need one counter-example

IN REALITY, ISSUES ARE OFTEN MUCH MORE COMPLEX.

to disprove the thesis. A 'softer' version would be: 'Most men drive too fast.' This claim would be much easier to justify. Watch out for simplistic overstatements – 'hard' generalisations – and don't be taken in by their rhetorical force.

7 TOP TRUMPS

My son has a pack of Top Trumps linked to a well-known car show. He loves playing Top Trumps with me because he knows all the data on every car, and he knows he can beat me without even trying. His favourite car (and mine) is the Koenigsegg Agera – it has the highest top speed; nothing can beat it.

People can play something like Top Trumps when they argue. They appeal to an authority which supposedly proves beyond doubt that they are right and you are wrong. Sometimes the Top Trump is vague: 'Scientists have proven that ...' Sometimes it will be more specific: 'Well, I think you'll find Stephen Hawking says ...' When somebody argues like this they are calling an expert witness to give account in their favour. If a brilliant scientist backs you up, who could possibly disagree? And there's something to that argument. Expert opinion does matter and we want to find out what the people who really know their stuff think.

To some degree, then, we have to rely on the testimony of

experts – unless their Top Trump is wrong. Take spinach as an example. It is widely believed to be a great source of iron – in the words of Popeye, 'I'm strong to the finish, 'cause I eats my spinach.' The truth is that the German chemist who calculated the amount of iron in spinach put his decimal point in the wrong place, thereby claiming spinach contains ten times the amount of iron that it does in fact have. Expert opinion is useful so long as we remember that it is possible even for experts to sometimes get it wrong.

8 PICK 'N' MIX ARGUMENTS

This fallacy is surprisingly common and happens when somebody makes selective use of the evidence to back up their case. In a way it's understandable – not many people have access to all of the evidence, let alone the time to weigh and sift it all. Linked to selective use of the evidence is the generalisation – that is moving from some observed data and applying it to the whole. Such an argument can be frequently seen or heard on the television or radio. For example, a radio phone-in show I listened to was discussing the issues surrounding immigration. One caller offered his pearls of wisdom: 'Every Eastern European

I meet – they're all criminals.' The unstated and implied conclusion was that every person from Eastern Europe is a criminal. Regardless of whether his statement of his own experience is true (which I doubt), the conclusion does not follow. Unfortunately, however, this is how many people think and reason on a daily basis.

Also related to the pick 'n' mix argument is avoiding the question altogether. Politicians are skilled in this. Someone once told me that politicians are trained in the 'ABC' of handling media questions. ABC stands for Acknowledge, Bridge, Communicate. In other words they are taught to acknowledge the question in a sentence, bridge across to what they really want to talk about, and then communicate what they want to say. In this way they avoid difficult questions and have a platform to sell their ideas. I don't know whether politicians really are trained in the ABC of media communication, but I've certainly seen something that looks like it in Prime Minister's Questions.

9 SHOOTING YOURSELF IN THE FOOT

Sometimes your own argument backfires on you. A good slapstick example of this is Wile E. Coyote, from the *Looney Tunes* cartoons, who habitually lays a trap for his prey, the

Road Runner, only to normally blow himself up with it. Here's another example:

> *Bob: 'There is no truth.'*
> *Vic: 'Is that true?'*
> *Bob: 'Well, there's no absolute truth.'*
> *Vic: 'Are you absolutely sure?'*
> *Bob: 'Truth is relative.'*
> *Vic: 'Is that a relative statement?'*

In each case Bob says something that is self-contradictory in its own terms. The statement 'There is no truth' is a statement about truth. The same applies to the other statements. If I were to say, 'All truth must be determined empirically', my problem is that we cannot determine the truth of my statement empirically. Therefore it fails as a statement of truth on its own terms.[18]

This sort of thing tends to happen when discussing big philosophical questions about God and religion. It's seen as tolerant and enlightened to say phrases such as, 'I think all the roads lead up the same mountain', or, 'Everyone makes their own journey, but we all end up in the same place.' It sounds lovely, right? However, implied within the statement is a fairly exclusive, absolute statement. The implication of the statement is that people

SOMETIMES YOUR OWN ARGUMENT BACKFIRES ON YOU.

who think there might be only one way up the mountain are close-minded, intolerant, and should be dealt with (normally by some sort of mockery or ostracism). Our society's idea of tolerance, it turns out, is intolerant of some points of view. The suggestion that all roads lead up the mountain is a suggestion about the right way (and therefore implicitly the wrong way). As an argument it shoots itself in the foot by proposing *the* right way to think – namely that there are many ways. What the argument claims is in fact denied in the premise.

10 RUNNING AROUND IN CIRCLES

'Circular reasoning' occurs when somebody uses the premise as both conclusion and evidence. For example, if I were to say, 'Intuition must decide moral dilemmas', you might legitimately ask, 'On what basis?' If I replied, 'Well, it just seems intuitive', I would have been caught in circular reasoning.

Actually, the truth is we all do this to some extent. Whichever of the TRIBES we cite as our authority is done so on a somewhat circular basis – if reason, it's because it seems reasonable; if society, it's because that's what everyone else does; if tradition, it's because that's what our forebears did; if a book, it's because that's what the book says. Circularity is to some degree unavoidable. Christians are often accused of this sort of circular reasoning because we believe the Bible based on its own testimony about itself. In reply we should affirm that everyone engages in circular reasoning where their ultimate authority is concerned. We can widen the circle, however, by bringing in other evidences. In fact thinking about a way through this problem takes us into the subject of the next chapter.

We need to be aware of these siren voices as we attempt to weigh up difficult ethical issues. It is so common for people to use emotion, personal attack, or slippery-slope arguments to attack straw men, present things as 'either-or', appeal to authority, and selectively use evidence. And when this happens it's easy to get swept along with the emotion, the rhetoric, and the crowd. Almost unthinkingly we can make rash decisions about big issues without ever stopping to do the hard work of thinking it through for ourselves.

4
WHERE DO WE GO FROM HERE?
A WAY THROUGH THE MAZE

In reality most of us flit between the authorities we listen to and employ a combination of them. And in truth most of us are primarily drawn to those authorities that allow us to believe or practise that which is in line with our existing desires. Some of us will major more on reason, some on intuition, some on past experience, and still others on a holy book. As we have seen, different issues push us more toward one authority, while other issues cause us to lean on another. Perhaps the most important question to ask of any of these is: 'On what basis do we trust them?' All appeals to authority necessitate a basis of trust and we have to consider why we have confidence in our authority sources. What characteristics should we look for in the authority sources on which we rely? I suggest there are three, as follows:

1 KNOWLEDGE

First, our authority source must have knowledge, particularly about our area of interest. I am, unfortunately, a complete ignoramus when it comes to cars. If anything goes wrong I need to find an expert – someone who actually knows what they're doing. Only someone who knows all about cars is able to tell me both the problem and the solution. If I have a medical problem, deciding to self-diagnose via Google is perhaps not the best approach. Again, I need someone who knows what they're doing; I need a qualified doctor.

When it comes to ethical issues it's not always obvious to whom we should turn. Ideally we'd love to find someone who understands the human condition and what's good or bad for us. If that authority was an expert in this field they would certainly be worth listening to, right?

2 GOODNESS

The second requirement of a trustworthy authority source is that they are good and not evil. We all know that it's not enough for the mechanic to know the problem and the solution; we also have to trust that he or she is a decent person, otherwise they could easily use their knowledge to rip us off. Dr Harold Shipman made headline news in 1998 for murdering a number of elderly patients in his care. He made home visits and administered fatally high doses of morphine, in one case in order to inherit £386,000.

So knowledge alone is not enough; we also need our authority to be good. If our 'authority' knows what's best yet tells us to do something else, that would obviously be a bad thing for us and others. We need an ultimate authority who knows all about our problem and the solution, and who can be trusted to be good in telling us that which is most beneficial to us, sometimes whether we like it or not. A good mechanic will tell me what I *need* to hear, not always what I *want* to hear! A good doctor likewise will tell me the truth even when its bad news.

This is crucially important when applied to ethical issues. There is a misconception in our current culture that to disagree with someone is to 'hate' them, and it may perhaps even amount to a 'hate crime'. Let's be clear on this. You can hate someone by telling them lies, even if you're telling them things they want to hear. And vice versa, you can love someone by telling the truth, even if you're telling them something they don't agree with. In fact to truly love someone you are obligated to tell them the truth. If I really believed that a certain course of action was not good for

KNOWLEDGE ALONE IS NOT ENOUGH.

you, and I didn't tell you, would I be loving you or not? Of course we need to be caring and considerate in the way in which we might disagree with others, but disagreement itself doesn't make someone a bigot. As one author states:

> Certain kinds of ethical decisions may be, perhaps, matters of individual choice or personal commitment ... but that fact need not remove the associated arguments from the sphere of public criticism ... the personal character of some ethical attitudes and decisions does not make them any less open to *rational discussion and criticism*.[1]

3 POTENCY

This brings us to the third thing we want from our trustworthy authority. We want them to act on their knowledge and their goodness. It's no good for my honest mechanic to rightly identify the problem and then to do nothing to fix it. Once my good doctor has identified my problem I want him to act on his findings. Think about it this way. Recently I was on holiday with my family on the south coast of England. We were walking along the beach by the beautiful Seven Sisters chalk cliffs. It's a wonderfully picturesque part of Britain's coastline, but it's also dangerous. As we walked along under the cliffs there were parts where large chunks of the cliff face had fallen away – some chunks of rock were the size of a family car. Now imagine we saw some kids playing at the foot of the cliffs, and at the same time we saw someone from the local authority walk by who began to shout at the kids to move. Why did he do that? Was he just being mean and spoiling their fun? No. He knew the cliff face was unstable and he knew that even a small rock falling could cause serious injury or death to them. Because he's a good citizen he recognised the danger they were in and cared enough to act. His knowledge and goodness led him to speak – to tell those children about what's good for them, bad for them, and the action they need to take.

So the three characteristics for a legitimate authority are knowledge, goodness, and potency. Knowledge and goodness without action isn't much use to anyone. Goodness and action without knowledge is well intentioned but may be misdirected. Knowledge and action without goodness leaves enacted evil as a real possibility. All three are crucial in determining whose voice we should listen to, particularly in difficult ethical questions.

THE SEARCH FOR A TRUSTWORTHY AUTHORITY

To take all of this back into the realm of thinking through difficult questions we now need to see if we can identify the sort of authority that has these three characteristics – knowledge, goodness, and power to act. Part of our problem as thinking beings is our own limitations and our finitude. We've seen that tradition, reason, intuition, experience, and society are both useful and limited. They can teach us true and useful things, but they can also get it spectacularly and disastrously wrong.

This is where this book perhaps gets controversial for you. Bear with me. Critically engage with what I have to say and see if, by the end, the argument is valid and sound. Before we arrive at the controversial bit, though, we need to remind ourselves of what makes for a good argument. An argument is 'valid' when the premises logically lead to the conclusion. An argument is 'sound' if the premises are actually true.[2] So, as we bear in mind all that we've seen so far, here's the argument I wish to defend: as a Christian my view is that we have an all-knowing, all-good, acting (speaking through his Word, the Bible) authority. The Bible claims that God has revealed himself to us as our good, wise, loving, and all-knowing creator. He (God) has revealed himself to us in his Word, the Bible, and therefore the Bible should be our ultimate authority. He is the one who not only has the right to be heard, but also knows all about what's best for us. Before you dismiss what I'm saying, hear me out.

In 2 Timothy 3:16 the apostle Paul says, 'All Scripture is God-breathed and is useful for teaching, rebuking, correcting and training in righteousness'. The apostle Peter, speaking about Scripture, says, 'For prophecy never had its origin in the human will, but prophets, though human, spoke from God as they were carried along by the Holy Spirit' (2 Peter 1:21). Jesus, in debate with his opponents, appeals to Scripture as his authority claiming, 'Scripture cannot be broken'[3] (John 10:35). In each case, Paul, Peter, and Jesus are referring to the Old Testament, so it's hugely important when Peter, in one of his letters, refers to Paul's writing too as Scripture (2 Peter 3:16). The writers of the Bible have an awareness that what they write is not simply human words, stories, letters, or reflections, but have come from God himself.[4] Bible writers

THE HOLY SPIRIT HAS BREATHED INTO THEIR OWN WORDS.

aren't inspired like Rembrandt or Vivaldi were inspired. The Holy Spirit has breathed into their own words to ensure that what they wrote was both fully human and fully divine. So when we pick up the Bible we are reading the words of an all-knowing, all-good, acting/speaking God who knows us better than we know ourselves, and knows what's good for us and what's bad for us. Of course we need to interpret the Bible carefully, and humans can misuse and abuse it for selfish reasons. Yet it remains God's message of love and concern to us for our good, and thus we need to listen to it, even when it disagrees with us or says things we don't find easy to hear. It's an act of God's love to tell us when we're harming ourselves!

NAVIGATING THE MORAL MAZE

When I was a kid I used to love visiting attractions that contained a maze – a real maze, with eight-foot high hedges. My brother and I would love to go sprinting in and see who could find their way to the centre (and then back out) first. As we ran around we could call out to one another to see how the other was getting on. Inevitably we'd go down a number of dead ends, double back, and try to find another way through. There was always the mix of excitement with fear – what if we got really lost? How would we ever get out? Occasionally, if we hit the same dead end several times, an irrational fear might come over us of dying in the maze. The counsellors have helped me deal with that now.

A few years ago we were on holiday with my mum and we stumbled across such a place. This one had wooden sides and at the centre was a crow's nest which you could climb up into to display your maze-navigating prowess to the watching parents. Most of us navigated the maze and found the centre within a few minutes. My mum, however, got well and truly lost, and couldn't figure her way either to the centre or back out to the entrance. The rest of us had been in, come out, and had an ice cream. We decided we probably shouldn't leave her

OUR ALL-SEEING EYES COULD POINT HER IN THE RIGHT DIRECTION.

there too long so a couple of us ventured back in, hoping not to suffer the same fate. After a while we found our way back to the centre, climbed the crow's nest, and could begin the process of guiding mum back to safety. It was only with our all-seeing eyes that we could point her in the right direction. From within the maze, at ground level, there was no way of my mum knowing which way to turn – just a helpless process of trial and error. Somehow we needed to get ourselves out and above the maze to see what was really going on, and therefore to help my mum.

When it comes to our thinking we suffer the same problem.

We, in ourselves, do not possess the all-seeing knowledge to navigate our way through the moral maze. Our various authorities are all working from the ground – reason, tradition, intuition, experience and society. Sometimes they lead us well; often we end up in dead ends. We can believe things that aren't true, and things may be true that we don't believe.[5] What we're interested here in is a *justified* true belief. What we need is someone who knows all, and sees all, to tell us where to go. The unique claim of Christianity is that God has sent us such a guide, and his name is Jesus. He comes from on high – he sees the whole picture – and knows which way we should be going. And he's left us a map to navigate with. It's called the Bible. The Bible itself claims to be God's Word. Jesus himself viewed

WHAT WE NEED IS SOMEONE WHO KNOWS ALL.

the Scripture as authoritative. It may seem old-fashioned to us, but if the claim is true, it means that God himself is the all-knowing, all-good guide, and his moral map is found within the Bible. Of course, as I've mentioned before, we need to interpret the Bible carefully, using various other tools – reason, tradition, Bible commentaries and so on – but fundamentally the only reliable guide for our thinking and living is the Word of God found in the pages of the Bible.

JESUS, THE SON OF GOD, IS OUR TRUE AUTHORITY

The most famous verse in the Bible is John 3:16: 'For God so loved the world that he gave his one and only Son, that whoever believes in him shall not perish but have eternal life.' The most crucial phrase in that verse is 'gave his … only Son'. John is claiming that Jesus represents God to humanity. If that claim is true then we have to listen to what Jesus says even when it jars with our tradition, reason, intuition, or culture. But do we have any evidence that such a claim is true? Could not John just be putting words onto the lips of Jesus after the event? Let me give you four pieces of evidence that demonstrate the truthfulness of John's claims.

1. JESUS' CLAIMS ABOUT HIMSELF

First, look at Jesus' own claims about himself. He claims to have existed before Abraham (John 8:58), who himself existed about 2000 years before Jesus was born. He claims to be 'one with the Father' (John 10:30), and tells his disciples that if they have seen him (Jesus) then they have seen the Father (John 14:9). And it wasn't just Jesus' followers who understood what Jesus was claiming. His opponents also understood exactly what he was getting at: 'For this reason they [the Jewish leaders] tried all the more to kill him; not only was he breaking the Sabbath, but he was even calling God his own Father, making himself equal with God' (John 5:18). Again later, when Jesus' opponents picked up rocks to chuck at him, Jesus asked them why and they replied, 'for blasphemy, because you, a mere man, claim to be God' (John 10:33).

Sometimes people say something along the lines of, 'I like Jesus – he seems to have been a good man; but I don't much like Christians or church.' If you really understand the things Jesus claims for himself he cannot be merely a good man. Imagine Boris Johnson or David Cameron claiming to be the Son of God. We would think they were uttering words of arrogance or the asylum. Jesus' outrageous claims make him a bad man, a mad man, or the God-man – and he can only be a good man if he's the last of these.[6]

2. THE MIRACLES OF JESUS

The second piece of evidence is the miracles of Jesus. He healed people who had been paralysed or blind for the entirety of their lives (John 5:1–9; 9:1–7); he fed 5000 people from only five small loaves and two small fish, and walked on water (John 6:1–24); he even managed to raise someone who'd been dead and entombed for four days (John 11:38–44).

But did he, though? I mean, really? To answer that question

we need to consider the reliability of our sources. The four gospel accounts (Matthew, Mark, Luke, and John) are written somewhere between just twenty-five and thirty-five years after the death of Jesus.[7] When the eyewitnesses of Jesus' life on earth begin to die out, their testimony is written down for future generations. To help us see the importance of these facts, let's think of a similar example. I'm writing this in the summer of 2015.

I REMEMBER GAZZA BALLING HIS EYES OUT.

If I go back twenty-five years I find myself in the summer of 1990 – Italia 90 and the football World Cup. I remember it well. I was ten years old and my parents let me stay up late to watch England's semi-final against Germany. I remember Gazza balling his eyes out when he was given the yellow card which meant he would miss the final, should England reach it; I remember Lineker's equaliser; I remember the penalty shoot-out with Chris Waddle blazing the ball into row Z and Pearcey smashing it down the middle and into the legs of the German keeper. Oh the pain of those memories! Yet if someone tried to rewrite Italia 90 to include all sorts of things that didn't really happen there are enough people around who could quickly discredit such an endeavour. The same is true of the historical accounts of Jesus' life. If they were untrue, given the time period within which they were written, they could have been quickly discredited. In addition the manuscript evidence for these accounts is so overwhelming that the events surrounding Jesus' life, death, and resurrection are the best attested in all of ancient history. The miracles happened, and they tell us that Jesus is who he claimed to be.

3. THE EVIDENCE OF JESUS' DEATH

The third piece of evidence is Jesus' death. It was remarkable for all sorts of reasons – the three hours of darkness from 12 to 3 p.m.; the tearing in two of the temple curtain; the breaking open of tombs, with those dead people being raised to life and coming out; and the highly unusual brevity with which Jesus actually died – this was no ordinary death.[8] When the centurion saw how Jesus died he exclaimed, 'Surely this man was the Son of God' (Mark 15:39). This centurion was no gullible halfwit. He was a hardened Roman soldier who made his living executing people. He knew what it was like to watch a man die a slow painful death. He'd have done it possibly hundreds of times. And yet, when he saw Jesus' death, he could not help but conclude that there was something radically different about the man crucified between two thieves.

4. JESUS' RESURRECTION

The fourth and final piece of evidence to consider is the resurrection. Jesus was undoubtedly dead. The Romans were good at killing people, and even if you could survive crucifixion (which you couldn't), infection would have got you in the tomb. So Jesus couldn't have fainted, swooned, passed out, gone into a coma or anything like that. He was most definitely dead. And yet, on the Sunday morning, the tomb was also definitely empty, as all the gospel accounts affirm.[9] Even Jesus' opponents couldn't deny this truth and instead attempted to pay off the soldiers to say someone stole the body (Matthew 28:11–15). And then Jesus began to appear to people – first to the women who had gone to Jesus' tomb (Matthew 28:8–9);[10] then to some disciples on the Emmaus road (Luke 24:13–32); then to the eleven remaining disciples (Luke 24:33–43);[11] and at one point to 500 people (1 Corinthians 15:6).

This isn't like the individual who swears they've seen Elvis. This is 500 people, at the same time, who claim to have seen him. Remember the time frame this is written in; there were plenty of people around who could have validated or discredited the claim. Remember too where Christianity is birthed: Jerusalem – the same place Jesus was killed. Surely, if Jesus had not risen to life

JESUS COULDN'T HAVE FAINTED, SWOONED OR PASSED OUT.

again, at some point an opponent would have pointed to where the body was, or a disciple would have cracked and pointed to where a body was hidden. It never happened. Christianity exploded across the Roman Empire over the next couple of centuries, and all but one of Jesus' disciples were martyred for their belief that they had seen Jesus risen from the dead.

These four reasons put together are good evidence for believing John's claim that God had sent his only Son, that Jesus represents God to humanity, and therefore that we need to listen to what he says. Jesus views the Bible as God's Word, and therefore that has to be our authoritative source in our reasoning and decision-making. As Tim Keller has said, 'If Jesus rose from the dead, then you have to accept all that he said.'[12] I have tried to present evidence to demonstrate that the premise (Jesus is the Son of God) is true. The evidence convinces me that the argument I've been presenting (Jesus is the Son of God, and therefore we need to listen to what he says) is valid and sound.

As I have repeatedly stated, tradition, reason, intuition, books, experience, and society at large are both helpful and limited in helping us think through ideas, values, and beliefs. We need an all-knowing, all-good, active foundation to be our ultimate authority. I find the evidence for Jesus compelling. He is the ultimate authority to which all the subservient authorities answer. He is the one to whom we need to listen.

5

A FEW WORKED EXAMPLES

I confess I'm extremely nervous about this next section. I've deliberately picked emotive issues to put this thinking to the test. It's also difficult in a medium such as the written word to fully capture nuance, expression, and emotion, but I'm going to try and address difficult issues with sensitivity as well as intellectual clarity. Remember, I'm not trying to tell you *what* to think; I'm interested in *how* we think through difficult issues. That said, I'll inevitably be giving my view on these issues, while inviting you – the reader – to reflect upon them for yourselves.

1 OTHER RELIGIONS

There is a popularly held opinion that I have heard countless times. It normally goes something like this: 'I like to think that we're all branches coming out from one trunk', or 'We're all just following different paths up the same mountain', or 'We all have a bit of the truth and we need to come together to learn from each other.' It's the six blind men all groping an elephant. Each one has a particular aspect of the whole and so – as the moral of the tale goes – we need to learn from each other. It sounds very enlightened, tolerant, kind, and loving to our fellow man. But let's get our six honest men to work.

WHO?

Tradition

Traditionally, in the United Kingdom, people have believed that Christianity is the only true religion. Following the Roman conquest of England nearly two millennia ago,

Christianity spread to Britain. Though initially a minority faith it became the religion of the state. Of course since then we have seen the influx of others with their own cultures and different traditional beliefs, so tradition pure and simple can't be decisive.

Reason

Logically speaking it is difficult to reconcile the idea that all religions lead to God with the religious beliefs themselves. Objectively speaking, they do believe contradictory things. For example, do humans die once and face judgement as Christianity teaches (Hebrews 9:27) or are they reincarnated as Hinduism teaches (Gita 2:22)? The only way to reconcile the contradictions is to affirm that a religion is as much in error as it is in truth. At this point we find *ourselves* determining what's true and false. So the reality is that rather than embracing true pluralism we're really just making up our pick 'n' mix religion according to ourselves, while dismissing the bits of the other religions we don't like.

Intuition

Intuition has been a powerful guiding force for lots of religious leaders. Ecstatic visionary experiences lie behind almost all of the major world religions. Unfortunately many of these visionary experiences are mutually contradictory, and so, as with tradition, are of limited value in determining whose truth is really true.

Book

Religious texts, as noted under 'reason' above, contain significant differences in terms of the person and nature of God, the way of salvation, and life after death. At this point we have to consider the evidence – the specific manuscript, history, and internal consistency of each religious text. We've argued that the historical accounts of Jesus' life, death, and resurrection give us good reason to trust that Jesus is the Son of God, and the Bible is the Word of God. For me, God's Word (Jesus and the Bible) are the authority we need to listen to on these questions.

Experience

Personal experience plays a large part in people's religious viewpoint. A meeting, a dream, a book, or any number of things can form our deepest-held beliefs. Yet, as with the other authorities, what are we to do with wildly differing experiences? How do we work out the divine from the demonic?

Society

Contemporary Western societies generally hold the opinion outlined above that belief systems are simply different roads up the same mountain, which will ultimately all arrive at the same destination.

WHY?

So why do we choose the authority we do on this question? Is it because of the way we've been brought up (tradition)? An incredible religious experience? Hard evidence, or just a 'sense' of the way things are? Or maybe a religious text, be that the Qur'an, the Bible, or whatever else? As we've already said, the evidence for Jesus is the reason that he is the authority to whom we should pay attention.

HOW?

How are we conducting our reasoning? Are we carefully considering the evidence? Are we aware of our own presuppositions? Or is it determined by who is shouting loudest in the debate?

The majority view of our culture – that all religions are different roads up the mountain and all have a bit of the truth – is an idea with little credible basis. Let's think about the mountain metaphor. To know that the majority view was right you'd have to be able to climb into a helicopter, fly up over the mountain of religions, take all the aerial photographs of the various roads

WHY DO WE CHOOSE THE AUTHORITY WE DO?

of religion terminating at the top, and present your evidence to the rest of the world. Yet we can't do that. We don't have the all-seeing eye to know that Buddha, Muhammad, and Joseph Smith (the founder of Mormonism) are all sat round enjoying one another's company in the next life. We simply cannot know that. It is pure speculation – wishful thinking, not critical thinking.

We need to listen to the one who has come to our world from outside, and who therefore knows about the origin and veracity of other religions – and that is Jesus.

WHAT?

What are we talking about really? Is it at root actually the idea that I ought to be free to choose my own beliefs – that nobody else should be able to tell me that something so intensely personal is wrong? Is there really a desire to find truth or just to assuage our own consciences as we face the brevity of life and the reality of eternity?

If we're serious about truth, purpose, and life eternal we need to pursue the evidence where it leads. Eternity is at stake – for us, for our friends, and for our family. Pursuing the 'nice' answer won't help if we're wrong. Truth is crucial if we're serious about loving one another, and discovering the divine object of our affection.

WHERE?

Where is this debate taking place for us? Well, it's in our culture. And seeing as we live on a multi cultural Island there is perhaps a heightened desire for us all to basically agree and get along. We need to be aware of the ways in which this will bias our thinking.

WHEN?

Twenty-first century Britain is the context of our thinking. Whatever has gone before is often deemed irrelevant, while the new is seen as most enlightened. As with the 'where?' question we need to be aware of the various ways in which our culture shapes our thinking.

Jesus said, 'I am the way and the truth and the life. No one comes to the Father except through me' (John 14:6). That is the authoritative word on other religions. I know it's not popular in modern Western society. It might not *feel* particularly nice. Yet we've seen good evidence that we should take seriously everything Jesus says. And Jesus' verdict is that he alone is the Son of God, representing God to us, and showing us the way to God and eternal life. If this is true it's the only loving thing to proclaim.

2 BEGINNING-OF-LIFE OR END-OF-LIFE ISSUES

Let's work back through our six honest serving-men:

WHO?

Tradition

Historically abortion and euthanasia have been viewed negatively in Britain's recent history (by which I mean the last 1000 years). Abortion was illegal up until 1967 and therefore all sorts of horrific back-street operations were carried out until then. Euthanasia is still (in 2016) illegal in Britain and historically suicide has been frowned upon. Only in more recent times have people debated whether euthanasia ought to be legalised on the grounds of compassion. As we've already said, tradition in and of itself proves little, but it should urge us to think carefully before making radical changes.

Reason

Many of the arguments around this subject look to reason and evidence. Questions abound and are hotly debated regarding the nature of personhood; when life begins; whether a foetus experiences pain; the competing rights of the baby versus the mother; the number of weeks when it becomes unacceptable to terminate; and so forth. At the other end of life's spectrum debates rage about the quality of palliative care; the right of the individual to determine their death; the potential unintended consequences of legalising euthanasia; and so on.

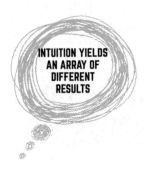

INTUITION YIELDS AN ARRAY OF DIFFERENT RESULTS

Much of the debate on both these issues comes down to the nature of personhood – when life begins, and who has the right to determine life's beginning and end. What makes me a person not to be murdered at twenty-four weeks and one day, but a foetus that may be terminated at twenty-four weeks? Why is termination legal if it happens *in utero* at twenty-four weeks but illegal if it happens *ex utero* at twenty-four weeks? If the infringement of one person's 'rights' by another legitimises termination, why not allow it at twenty-five weeks, or one year, or sixty-five years? This debate more than any other uncovers some astonishingly sloppy thinking and arbitrary lawmaking. The sorts of questions raised above illustrate the fact that logically inconsistent conclusions drawn from reason alone should compel us to urge a great deal more caution in this whole area.

Intuition

Like reason, intuition yields an array of different results. Many instinctively feel it's a woman's right to terminate an unwanted pregnancy, and it's the individual's right to determine when and how they wish to end their life. (The whole area of rights is another, much bigger issue.) Yet just as many people take the opposite view – termination is not the termination of a pregnancy but of a person, and we don't get to decide how and when we die.

Intuition thus leaves us with a relative morality on this question – everyone must do what they see fit. It's just that there's quite a lot at stake for people to be playing God. As with reason, there can also be inconsistent intuition, examples of which have been seen in recent news stories. One story covered the burning of aborted foetuses to heat hospitals and another covered the selling of foetal body parts.[1] The fact that these stories made front page news is interesting. If foetuses aren't real persons then why not use them for fuel or sell the component parts? Yet people were outraged at these incidents, which demonstrates that we don't really believe foetuses aren't persons.

Book

Almost all religious texts would argue personhood is a

gift of God, and it is his prerogative to give and take away life, not ours. That's not to say there isn't a category of lawful killing (for example, in war or criminal punishment – though that too is a whole other debate), but that abortion or euthanasia (and suicide) fall into the 'unlawful' killing category. As argued above (we don't need to rehearse the argument every time) there are good reasons for making the Bible our authority in these questions.

Experience

This is where the various positions often make their case most forcefully. Women who have had abortions will sometimes express something akin to pride in the exercise of their rights, or they will express great remorse and regret.[2] Happy, fulfilled children with Down's Syndrome are adverts for pro-life campaigns.[3] At the other end of life people relate stories of either excellent palliative care, or terrible suffering. These issues are clearly emotive and both sides of the debate need to exercise great empathy. But as we have said previously love for someone else does not necessarily mean agreement, and disagreement does not necessarily mean hate. These issues are so important that we have to be able to wrestle through issues with clarity and care.

Society

On both of these issues it would be fair to say that society is divided. Many people don't like talking openly about them because opinion is divided and views are often strongly held. It would probably be fair to say that, at present, a slight majority are in favour of abortion, and a slight minority are in favour of euthanasia. In another generation I would not be surprised to see the majority of society in favour of both. But as we've tried to demonstrate numerous times already, being in the majority or minority is not a necessary or sufficient indicator of being either right or wrong.

WHY?

Thinking about which authority we favour takes us onto our second question – why? Why are we choosing that authority (or combination of authorities)? On what basis do we trust them or think they are telling the right story? Are we aware of our own biases or the effect of our culture upon us? These two questions are fundamental and worth returning to often. On any issue keep asking, 'Who says?' and,

ON ANY ISSUE KEEP ASKING, 'WHO SAYS?'

'Why do I/we favour them?' As we've outlined above, God's Word is the Bible because Jesus says so, and the evidence for him being the Son of God is compelling.

HOW?

Are we reasoning properly and carefully, or are we just following gut instinct or the crowd? Much of the method in the arguments for or against abortion and euthanasia appeals to experience, and, it could be argued, employs

THE REAL DEBATE – IS AROUND LIMITS ON PERSONAL AUTONOMY.

science to attempt to confirm the view already held. Reasoning in these areas is seldom dispassionate; rather it is fierce and impassioned. As a consequence the thinking is often sloppy. Many of the fallacies listed in chapter three can be seen in these debates – an emotive appeal; talk of a slippery slope; a straw man; generalisations; character assassination; and pick 'n' mix arguments. And both sides of these debates are equally guilty. Christians need to consider carefully what God's Word has to say about these complex issues.

WHAT?

What actually is the issue here? Is it human rights, dignity, liberty, or something else? Is this ultimately a desire to be God – making our own rules to suit the varying circumstances of our own lives? Terming the issue one of 'choice' clouds the issue since, if we attributed personhood to the unborn, then we are talking about a choice no-one thinks is on the table. Are we really interested in what's best for others or is there something deeper and perhaps murkier going on in our hearts and heads?

The debate is often defined in terms of the personal right to decide. Where abortion is concerned the decision-making is far more concerned with the rights of the mother, rather than the rights of the unborn child. Advocates of the mother's right to choose reveal the heart of the issue – the real debate – is around the extent and limits on personal autonomy. Babies are called 'foetuses' because that denies them access to basic human rights. The hard question to face is whether our desire for autonomy ultimately trumps the interests of others. End-of-life issues are more complex where there is often a genuine desire not to be a burden to others, or for loved family and friends to have to watch us die a slow and painful death.[4]

WHERE?

We must consider where this debate is happening. For us the discussion is UK-based, but it might look very different in Switzerland or Swaziland. Is there anything we need to be aware of about our culture that is shaping this discussion?

WHEN?

For us this is, obviously, a 21st-century discussion. Again, do we think our wisdom should hold for every age, and every place, or is it just our passing culture? Is the previous generation allowed to influence our viewpoint, and how would we feel if future generations reversed our decisions and deemed us unenlightened and barbaric? The fact that our culture's acceptance of abortion is in the overwhelming historical and geographical minority is not decisive in terms of the rights and wrongs, but it should urge us to be incredibly careful in our choices.

The contours of this debate surround personhood, rights, and dignity. The Bible says that personhood is, from God's perspective, eternal. Psalm 139:16 says, 'Your eyes saw my unformed body; all the days ordained for me were written in your book before one of them came to be.' Sometimes people say, 'Life begins at conception.' I think the Bible says personhood, from God's perspective, exists in eternity. God

OUR DIGNITY IS DERIVED FROM THE AUTHOR OF LIFE.

sees us, knows us, and has ordained our days before we were even a glint in our daddy's eye.[5] Since God is the author of all life, any taking of life falls into the category of either lawful or unlawful in God's eyes. Examples of the lawful taking of life would include those prescribed for the state or soldier. Abortion, suicide, and euthanasia, biblically speaking, are in the category of an unlawful taking of life. Human beings are made in the image of God (Genesis 1:27) and are therefore accorded great dignity. Our worth is not defined by whether our birth is welcomed or by our function or ability – our dignity is derived from the author of life.

3 SAME-SEX MARRIAGE

Let us once more repeat the exercise already outlined above:

WHO?

First, who gets to speak to this issue? Let's walk through the various contenders:

Tradition

Our culture has, historically, defined marriage as being between a man and a woman. Our parents' and our grandparents' generation would have concurred with the tradition of our culture. Of course traditions can be wrong. The Indian tradition of widow-burning is not justified on the basis of tradition. So tradition, while noteworthy, cannot be decisive.

Reason

What does reason dictate? In this case, not a great deal. There are numerous scientific studies debating whether sexuality is determined by nature or nurture, or a combination. Additionally there is some research into the stability, longevity, and fidelity in same-sex relationships, and their effect on children brought up in such environments. Various research studies are being used as evidence by both sides of the debate. As the experts in various fields can cast the argument either way, reason may not be all that helpful in this case.

Intuition

Gut feeling is likewise tricky here. For some people their strong feeling is that marriage ought to be between a man and a woman; for others that feels restrictive and narrow-minded. Recently the US legalised same-sex marriage. Social media lit up with the hashtag '#lovewins'. But does it really? Do we want to condone infidelity in the name of 'love'? Would we want to legalise polygamous marriage in the name of 'love' if all parties were consenting? Intuition is constantly moving the moral goalposts and so cannot be conclusive where people's consciences differ.

Book

For most religions marriage is between a man and a woman. But for many people that book is irrelevant or untrue, and therefore cannot be a determinative factor in such a debate. For the Christian, the Bible is the place we must look to in order to come to a position on what God thinks of the issue, and therefore same-sex marriage is wrong.

Experience

For many gay people (and friends of gay people) their experience is hugely important. They want to have the same access to marriage as heterosexual couples. Their general experience is one of abuse, exclusion, ridicule, and marginalisation, and marriage is another institution which excludes and reinforces negative attitudes toward gay people. However, people who have argued for a traditional definition of marriage have likewise been subjected to abuse and ridicule. Do we then decide on who feels more strongly, or who has suffered more abuse and ridicule? While no-one wishes to trivialise people's experience and feeling, one community's experience cannot be the definitive factor.

THE MAJORITY VIEW IS NOT NECESSARILY THE RIGHT VIEW.

Society

A recent YouGov poll suggests that the majority of Britons are in favour of same-sex marriage.[7] This is really the flipside of the tradition argument. Just as society past can be wrong, so society present can be wrong. The majority view is not necessarily the right view.

WHY?

Which 'authority' do you plump for in this debate? Perhaps a combination? And then, why them? Is it because 'We've always done it this way', or 'Because it seems unreasonable to do otherwise', or 'It feels right', or 'This is what most people want'? As above, there are good reasons for letting God's Word be our authority in determining the answers to difficult questions.

HOW?

On what basis are these decisions being made? Evidence? Intuition? Majority rule? Are there some voices shouting louder than others who dominate the agenda? Christians can be as guilty as anyone when it comes to poor reasoning on this issue. We too appeal to tradition, or a 'sense' of what is right (whichever side of the debate you're on). Perhaps most disturbing are Christians who claim to appeal to the Bible but misinterpret or misapply the Bible. This area, like the others, requires a good methodology in our hermeneutics. Interpreting the Bible in its historical and literary context, understanding the flow of an argument and the meaning of terms, and appreciating the history of interpretation can all help us to approach the Bible in a careful and responsible manner.

WHAT IS THE REAL ISSUE AT STAKE HERE?

WHAT?

What is the real issue at stake here? Is it equality, liberty, justice, or all of the above? The difficulty is that if the issue is liberty or equality, then the path should be opened up to polygamy or even bestiality. If it's justice, then we suppose that in denying same-sex marriage a crime is committed against a victim in which a right has been denied. But a right to what exactly? An institution, a certificate, a ceremony, or happiness? Part of the difficulty in this debate is defining terms. What exactly is being argued over? I suspect that, in common with the beginning- and end-of-life issues, there is a desire for autonomy – the freedom to do what we like without fear of reproach. It's a debate about freedom and authority. The discussion reveals a desire for humans to be their own gods with everyone doing what is right in their own eyes.

WHERE?

Where is this debate taking place? Is this legislation for every place or just our land? If it's just convenient for us, can it rightly be termed a justice issue? Should we campaign in other places for similar legislation? Or would that be an imposition on that sovereign state's liberty? Can one place dictate to another place or people group issues of right and wrong? If so, what makes us think we have the moral high ground? Are we smarter or more enlightened than other people groups, or would that be simply another instance of imperial arrogance?

WHEN?

In what era is this issue a live one? Is it something for our day or is this an absolute for all times? As above, is this convenient for our situation or should it be imposed as an eternal absolute value and statute? Again, can we dictate what the next generation should think? How do we feel about past generations' views on the issue? In short, are we talking absolute or relative moral authority? If it's relative, then fine (well, not fine really) – but you need to be aware of the implications of the position: you can have *no* moral absolutes. If you want absolute moral values then we'll have to look for such things beyond the whims and wills of ourselves, our day, our culture, and our politicians.

Let's work though this issue even more by looking at a specific incident. On the 19 May 2015 Ashers Bakery, in Northern Ireland, was found guilty of discrimination for refusing to bake a cake iced with the message 'Support gay marriage'. Whichever side of the debate you come down on, some of the comments made by the judge and the prosecuting QC are most interesting. Consider these statements by Judge Isobel Brownlie:

- *'The defendants are entitled to hold and manifest their religious beliefs in accordance with the law'* – that is absolutely right and fine.

- *'While the defendants have a right to religious beliefs they are limited as to how they manifest them'* – that is fair enough. I might have a deeply held belief that all left-handed people ought to be forcibly trained to be right-handed. The law does limit the extent to which I wish to practise my convictions, and that's a good thing.

- *To do otherwise* [i.e. not limit manifestation of religious belief] *would be to let religion dictate the law.'* Now, here's where it gets thought-provoking. Upon what basis do we decide what goes in the statute book? If it's upon 'no particular basis', then the law is arbitrary and the state a tyrant. If it is on some basis, then what exactly dictates that? Common sense? Tradition? The will of the majority? The will of the elite? Reason and history testify that these are not necessarily trustworthy. Nevertheless, say you choose whichever you favour but now ask on what basis those authorities function.

PUSH HARD ENOUGH AND THE ANSWER WILL BE 'BELIEF'.

What is their epistemological grounding? Push hard enough and the answer will be 'belief' – belief in moral categories of right and wrong; belief in the value of human beings, animals, and green spaces; belief in the appropriateness of justice and punishment. You can't run empirical investigation on those things – they are convictions or beliefs, held in faith by one or more people. In other words 'religion' (which is 'belief') *does* dictate law, if the law is to be based on something and not nothing. So the secular state isn't neutral, and the belief- (religion-) based law is choosing to uphold one set of beliefs against another – which precisely is a hierarchy of rights: the very thing the state is trying to avoid.

Leaving aside a discussion of the benefits and problems of the 2010 Equality Act, we need to see what's actually going on with this legislation. It prohibits the refusal of goods and services based on gender, race, religious belief, and so on. The law, based on its fundamental beliefs, discriminates against someone for discriminating against someone based on their beliefs. Now to some degree this is necessary and inevitable if you want law based on something, and not simply anarchy. But perhaps realising what's going on, and getting it out in the open, would actually allow a much greater degree of liberty and debate within the system. Personally I'm happy with belief-based law that criminalises discrimination against people – it accords with my beliefs. But I'd also like to see that belief-based law allow me freedom not to be involved in the endorsement of beliefs with which I disagree.

THE STATE IS EVERY BIT AS 'BELIEF-BASED' AS THOSE THEY SEEK TO PUNISH.

If we return to the Ashers ruling we can then perceive the possible unintended consequences of it. Must a gay baker be compelled by law to decorate a cake with a message against same-sex marriage if he doesn't want to? It seems to me that the proposed 'conscience clause' is a good idea that would benefit all. A Polish T-shirt printer would be at liberty to refuse to print a T-shirt with a BNP slogan on it. A feminist web designer would be at liberty to refuse to design a website for a sexist magazine. And an atheist printer would be at liberty to refuse to print my Christian tract. Of course all three are also at liberty to accept the work. It's their choice. It's how the *free* market should work. Yet a 'conscience clause' with regard to the endorsement and promotion of beliefs within the current Equality Act would both protect against discrimination against persons and protect the liberty of conscience of service providers. After all, the notion of the state coercing and compelling the sort of transactions outlined above, and criminalising those that refuse to comply, is alarming – especially since, as we have seen, the state is every bit as 'belief-based' as those they seek to punish.

To conclude on this issue, the Bible God creates male and female as equal but complementary partners in the stewardship of creation (including procreation). Any deviation from this pattern is viewed negatively – whether that be polygamy, adultery, bestiality, or homosexuality. The twisting of God's pattern for marriage and gift of sex is a symptom of rejecting God's rule over humanity. Romans 1 makes it clear that homosexuality is the exchange of truth for lie[6] – something that is ultimately bad for us, as it's a failure to love God and love one another rightly. This view of homosexuality in our culture is clearly unattractive, yet, if it's true, it is the only loving thing to say; anything else would be a harmful lie, however good it may feel.

We have to address this and all other questions carefully. They are undoubtedly emotive. Yet, in thinking them through, we have to ask on what basis we make moral judgements, and then why *our* basis is most preferable. Failure to engage at this deeper level results in all the mud-slinging, hate-inducing, shouting matches we see.

THE WORD OF AN ALL-KNOWING, ALL-GOOD, ALL-LOVING GOD

Let's suppose that the 'who' is an all-knowing, all-good, all-loving God who reveals himself to his creatures in his 'book' (the Bible). The Bible is God's good gift – a knowledgeable word from our creator about how we should live and what's good for us. We'd then learn that God set up a good created order for men and women to flourish. We'd also see that human beings have taken God's good gifts and, effectively, have drawn all over them in felt-tip pen, using them in ways they weren't supposed to be used, resulting in broken relationships with each other, creation, and, more seriously, with God. We've been told too by that same Word that God lovingly sent his Son to bring forgiveness and cleansing to all who turn to him. This could only be achieved by the costly sacrifice of Jesus dying on the cross to take the punishment we deserve, in our place. To all who turn back to God he's given his Spirit to help us live our lives according to his perfect pattern, and one day he'll remake our broken world and reveal a beautiful new creation in which those who love him will live forever.

JUSTICE IS ABOUT DOING WHAT IS RIGHT IN GOD'S EYES.

It is absolutely right for God to speak to our issues since he has revealed himself as all-knowing, all-good, and all-loving. He has the sovereign right, the knowledge, and perfect concern for us that makes him the perfect authority to speak on such issues. He speaks to us as a Father with both firmness and tenderness, seeking only our best. God speaks to the various inter-related issues – justice, liberty, equality, and happiness. Justice is about doing what is right in God's eyes, not our own; liberty is about the freedom to live according to God's ways and standards, not to exercise our own perceived rights (however keenly felt); equality is about our value before God as image-bearers, not our entitlement to grasp a status that goes against God's good, created order for us; and happiness is found in relationship with him first and foremost, which manifests itself in a relationship of trust and obedience, even where that makes tough calls on our wants and desires.

And because God is eternal his Word to us comes to every time and every place. Of course, as I have mentioned several times, we need to rightly interpret and apply the Bible – some parts of the Bible do speak to particular peoples in particular times and places – but nevertheless the eternal moral character of God is revealed clearly to us. And God gives us his Word not to spoil our fun and make us miserable but so that we might live life to the full in harmonious relationship with him and one another.

CONCLUSION

To return to where we started the book, as I sat in that room under the heat of the sun pouring through the window, and under the heat of the questions pouring in my direction, I felt as though I didn't have an adequate framework to begin to address such difficult issues. I thought I had some things I wanted to say, but no ordered way of thinking through them. This is an attempt to provide a sort of matrix through which to process difficult issues. Of course possessing a framework is not the same as possessing the answer. The hard work has only just begun. But my hope is that by having a framework to work with I, along with others, can begin to come to a more measured and informed opinion. Rather than shooting from the hip, together we can reflect on different perspectives. Rather than having clever answers, we can help people ask good questions. We can see bad arguments and appreciate good ones. We can be aware of our own dispositions and preconceptions. A step back may actually be a step forward.

In our fast-paced world we seldom pause for thought and reflection. We love everything to be ours in an instant – instant credit, instant information, and instant gratification, and for me still instant coffee and instant noodles too. But instant answers are often wrong answers. As H.L.

Mencken once said, 'There is always an easy solution to every human problem – neat, plausible, and wrong.'[1] Nor are difficult issues resolved through gut feeling, majority opinion, pithy quotes, or the thoughts of others. The six honest serving-men need to do some work – long, hard, laborious work – if we are to listen and respond with care, concern, and credibility. And we need to find (if we haven't yet) a trustworthy moral compass – one that always points us in the right direction, even when the terrain looks rocky.

The 2011 film *Margin Call* charts the story of a Wall Street investment bank facing the beginnings of the financial crisis of 2007–08. Their only option is a fire sale – to sell all their essentially worthless assets in a day. Their reputation will be ruined and their careers over, not to mention the

HOW DO WE DETERMINE WHAT IS RIGHT?

damage that will be done to those who buy these worthless assets. But for the ruthless executive, John Tuld (played by Jeremy Irons), it's the only way to save their own skin, regardless of the cost to others. The floor head Sam Rogers (Kevin Spacey) wrestles with the ethics of what he's being asked to do. His junior colleague Peter Sullivan at one point in the film asks him, 'Are you sure it's the only or right thing to do?' to which Rogers replies, 'For whom?'

How do we determine what is right? We need a trustworthy moral authority for the biggest and most difficult questions of life. We need to trust in an all-knowing, all-good, all-loving, all-wise moral authority who, like a Father with his children, challenges us when we err, comforts us in our failure, and sets us on the right course once again. His name is Jesus.

EPILOGUE

There was once a man who owned a beautiful estate which he and his family enjoyed very much. One day the man had to travel overseas for business and wouldn't be back for some time. He entrusted the care of the estate to his children. They were welcome to have parties and invite others as long as they observed some basic rules.

In the days and weeks which followed many came and stayed at the estate enjoying all it had to offer. But after a while the children began to worry about what their friends might think of their father and his rules. They loved their father and they wanted their friends to love him too. But some of his rules seemed a bit old-fashioned and out of date. They talked, reflected, and decided that some of their father's rules reflected his own generation – a different era where attitudes were different. So they changed some of those rules (or removed them altogether) to bring them up to date. Some of the rules were difficult to understand and they figured that if their father were there he wouldn't mean them quite as they read, so they edited or removed those too. And some of the rules

SOME OF HIS RULES SEEMED OUT OF DATE.

at first glance seemed a bit stern – a bit unaccepting, if you will – so they found new ways to explain what they *really* meant. After all, the important thing was to get their friends to come and enjoy the party, and love their father for his generosity as much as they did. No-one will do that if there are too many rules or the landlord seems a bit fuddy-duddy.

And so one day the father returned to find his estate not quite as beautiful as he'd left it, and to find that people had ignored the rules he carefully gave. Of course those dwelling on the estate were a bit surprised to find the landlord not at all like they imagined him – not at all like the children had presented him. He was a bit more conservative and a lot less liberal than they'd been led to believe. The father they so admired didn't, as it turned out, exist. And the trespassers were quickly removed, much to their dismay. They hadn't meant to break any rules. The children simply hadn't told them the whole picture. The children would later have to give their own account to their father.

A few of the new estate dwellers, however, were allowed to stay. They'd been tucked away in a little room. They had read the rules for themselves and decided it best to keep them. They were labelled old-fashioned killjoys: 'If only they had the imagination to see what the rules really meant,' said the rest. But they held fast. Having read the rules, they considered why the father might have given them. They didn't understand everything and wondered about this or that. Yet they decided that as it was the landlord's estate, he probably knew better than they did why the rules were for their good. So while the disobedient children were allowed to stay, it was the faithful estate dwellers who were now entrusted with its administration.

And those who didn't mess with the landlord's rules lived happily ever after.

HOW CAN WE START AGAIN WITH THE 'LANDLORD'?

God's world and God's Word are great gifts to us, yet often we live our lives without letting him be the true Lord of every part of us. If you want to surrender your life to him, as your Saviour and King, it's as simple as ABC.

'A' stands for 'admit' you've spent too long running from God and ignoring him. Your choices and actions mean that you are out of right relationship with him. The essence of sin is saying, 'Shove off, God. I'm in charge. No to your ways.' And you need to admit that fact, own it, and say sorry to God for the way you've treated him. The Bible uses the word 'repentance', which means 'to turn around'. Repentance is about turning away from your running and rebellion, and instead returning to God in humility, and asking for his forgiveness. This isn't something you do once, but is rather the ongoing posture of the Christian.

You need to admit your sin and keep turning from it, you should say sorry for it and every day keep turning to God.

'B' stands for 'believe' that God will forgive you because of what Jesus has already accomplished on the cross for us all. Jesus lived a perfect life on earth and therefore is the only human who has not deserved God's punishment. Yet he died as our substitute, in our place, bearing the just punishment of God against our sin so that we don't have to. Becoming a Christian (a follower of Jesus) isn't about trying harder to be a better person, in the hope that God might be favourable toward you. Becoming a Christian is about 'admitting' your sin, and 'believing' that if you trust in Jesus' sacrifice in your place, you can really, truly, fully know forgiveness.

'C' stands for 'commit' to following Jesus in love and obedience. When you become a Christian you don't pray a prayer of commitment then live how you like, continuing to ignore the God who gave his Son for you. That would be a terrible way to treat God and his incalculably immense gift of grace. A Christian is someone who, in response to this grace, wants to live in a way that pleases God. This honours him, and is good for us.

In one sense becoming a Christian might seem a massive and scary step. And Jesus did describe following him as carrying your own cross. It won't be easy, and it's not something you should do lightly or thoughtlessly. Yet, on the other hand, it's the easiest thing in the world to do. There's no need for a special person, place, or ritual to perform. You can talk to God right where you're sat, and he promises to hear you, forgive you, and begin a work of transformation in you. You might find the following prayer helpful if you're struggling to think of what to say:

Father in heaven,

I'm sorry for the many ways in which I've ignored you and rebelled against you.

I believe that you sent Jesus to die in my place.

I trust wholly in the cross for forgiveness.

I want to follow you.

I want you to be my Saviour and Lord

From this day on.

Amen.

FURTHER READING

Bowell, Tracy and Kemp, Gary, *Critical Thinking: A Concise Guide* (third edition; London: Routledge, 2009).

Butterworth, John and Thwaites, Geoff, *Thinking Skills: Critical Thinking and Problem Solving* (second edition; Cambridge: CUP, 2013).

Carswell, Roger, *Before you say 'I don't believe'* (Leyland: 10Publishing, 2014).

Carswell, Roger, *Grill a Christian* (Leyland: 10Publishing, 2011).

Fisher, Alec, *Critical Thinking: An Introduction* (Cambridge: CUP, 2001).

Hodges, Wilfrid, *Logic: An Introduction to Elementary Logic* (Reproduced; London: Penguin, 1991).

Keller, Timothy, *The Reason for God* (New York: Dutton, 2008).

Salter, Martin, *What's It All About?* (Leyland: 10Publishing, 2013).

Thouless, R.H. and Thouless, C.R., *Straight & Crooked Thinking* (Hodder: London, 2011).

Toulmin, Stephen, Rieke, Richard and Janik, Allan, *An Introduction to Reasoning* (second edition; New York: Macmillan, 1984).

Warburton, Nigel, *Thinking from A to Z* (third edition; London: Routledge, 2009).

NOTES

INTRODUCTION

[1] Tom Wright, *Virtue Reborn* (London: SPCK, 2010), p. 135.

[2] McNeese says, 'There were hundreds of thousands of slaves in America at the end of the eighteenth century. Most of those living in bondage were held in the Southern states, where slavery had taken root and flourished by the end of the 1600s.' Tim McNeese, *The Revolutionary War* (Dayton: Milliken, 2003), p. 38.

[3] For evidence of this, see Philip Jenkins' book *The Great and Holy War* (Oxford: Lion Hudson, 2014). The slogan *Gott mit uns* (translated 'God with us') was inscribed on German soldiers' belt buckles.

[4] Wilfrid Hodges, *Logic: An Introduction to Elementary Logic* (reproduced; London: Penguin, 1991), p. 15.

[5] Tracy Bowell and Gary Kemp, *Critical Thinking: A Concise Guide* (third edition; London: Routledge, 2009), p. 23.

[6] Butterworth and Thwaites define critical thinking as 'thinking about thinking'. John Butterworth and Geoff Thwaites, *Thinking Skills: Critical Thinking and Problem Solving* (second edition; Cambridge: CUP, 2013), p. 2.

1. SIX HONEST SERVING-MEN

[1] A good example can be viewed here: http://blogs.new.spectator.co.uk/2015/11/theres-absolutely-nothing-polite-about-political-correctness/. Cited 25 November 2015.

[2] It was interesting to observe that one group of cinemas banned the recent Church of England Lord's Prayer advert, entitled 'Just Pray', because they were worried it might offend somebody.

[3] Alec Fisher, *Critical Thinking: An Introduction* (Cambridge: CUP, 2001), p. 2.

[4] John Dewey, *How We Think* (Massachusetts: Heath & Co., 1909), p. 9.

[5] The book could be explicitly religious, like the Bible, Qur'an, Book of Mormon, or Bhagavad Gita; it may be more ideas-based, like Charles Darwin's *The Origin of Species* or Karl Marx and Frederick Engels' *The Communist Manifesto*.

[6] For those that like mnemonics the initial letters of those six spell the word 'tribes', which may help you remember it. We can then ask ourselves which of the 'tribes' gets to speak.

[7] This was seen, for example, in the 2015 UK general election where questions were raised over the merits of proportional representation versus first past the post as an electoral system.

[8] See http://www.independent.co.uk/news/world/africa/british-man-jailed-for-committing-homosexual-acts-in-morocco-9775471.html. Cited 3 December 2014.

[9] See the full story on the BBC website: http://www.bbc.co.uk/news/world-africa-33662230. Cited 6 November 2015.

2. TRIBES: THE COMPETING AUTHORITIES

[1] For more on the relationship between rationalism and empiricism see http://plato.stanford.edu/entries/rationalism-empiricism/#1.1

[2] I know some pedants will wish to point out that actually there are subtle variations based on altitude and purity but, for the purposes of the illustration, pipe down!

[3] Chip and Dan Heath, *Switch: How to Change Things When Change is Hard* (London: Random House, 2011).

[4] Martin Salter, *What's It All About?* (Leyland: 10publishing, 2013).

[5] See http://www.therichest.com/rich-list/most-influential/the-10-most-influential-books-ever-written/. Cited 30 July 2015.

[6] Bertrand Russell, 'On Denoting', in Mind 14 (1905), pp. 479–93. Available online at http://bactra.org/Russell/denoting/

[7] Michael Polanyi and Harry Prosch, *Meaning* (Chicago: University of Chicago Press, 1976), p. 61.

[8] George Santayana, *The Life of Reason: Reason in Common Sense* (New York: Scribner's, 1905), p. 284.

[9] See http://www.theguardian.com/society/2014/nov/29/i-helped-my-best-friend-to-die-euthanasia. Cited 5 December 2014.

[10] Ted Turnau, *Popologetics: Popular Culture in Christian Perspective* (New Jersey: P&R, 2012), p. 21.

[11] Ibid.

[12] R.H. Thouless and C.R. Thouless, *Straight & Crooked Thinking* (Hodder: London, 2011), p. 87.

3. THE ALLURE OF THE SIREN VOICES

[1] Fuller lists can be found in John M. Frame, *The Doctrine of the Knowledge of God* (New Jersey: P&R, 1987), pp. 278–301; Peter S. Williams, *A Faithful Guide to Philosophy* (Milton Keynes: Paternoster, 2013), pp. 41–65; and http://en.wikipedia.org/wiki/List_of_fallacies

[2] The examples that follow are taken from Bowell and Kemp, *Critical Thinking*, pp. 202–09.

[3] See http://tvtropes.org/pmwiki/pmwiki.php/Main/ChewbaccaDefense

[4] You can see Fry's comments here: https://www.youtube.com/watch?v=-suvkwNYSQo

[5] A good and measured response can be found here: http://www.christiantoday.com/article/stephen.fry.says.god.is.capricious.mean.minded.stupid.but.lets.not.get.angry/47174.htm

6 As an example, think of a parent taking a toddler for a vaccination. The toddler has no idea why the parent is allowing a total stranger to stab them in the backside. But the parent knows. In the same way, is it possible that there might be a higher mind that understands things we do not?

7 This was true, famously, of John Major, the prime minister of the UK between 1990 and 1997.

8 Butterworth and Thwaites, *Thinking Skills*, p. 52.

9 See James F. Haggerty, *In the Court of Public Opinion* (Chicago: ABA, 2009), pp. 11–13.

10 Haggerty, *In the Court of Public Opinion*, p. 13.

11 Nigel Warburton, *Thinking from A to Z* (third edition; London: Routledge, 2009), p. 124.

12 I'm not suggesting you should vote UKIP by the way – that's up to you – I'm simply encouraging you to watch out for the 'guilt by association' attack.

13 See http://www.bbc.co.uk/news/blogs-the-papers-32822057. Cited 21 November 2015.

14 John Frame uses the example 'Have you stopped beating your wife?', noting whichever way you answer you incriminate yourself. Frame, *The Doctrine of the Knowledge of God*, p. 295.

15 Bertrand Russell, 'On Denoting', in Mind 14 (1905), pp. 479–93. Available online at http://bactra.org/Russell/denoting/

16 See http://www.independent.co.uk/news/uk/politics/david-cameron-just-branded-a-lot-of-people-terrorist-

sympathisers-and-people-arent-happy-a6756776.html. Cited 4 December 2015.

[17] Bowell and Kemp, *Critical Thinking*, pp. 36–50.

[18] See the 'road runner tactic' (https://www.youtube.com/watch?v=r3Y-fOl086I) cited in Williams, *A Faithful Guide to Philosophy*, p. 43.

4. WHERE DO WE GO FROM HERE?

[1] Stephen Toulmin, Richard Rieke, and Allan Janik, *An Introduction to Reasoning* (second edition; New York: Macmillan, 1984), p. 416 (italics original). This point cuts both ways, for those who do not or indeed do hold to religious convictions.

[2] A further distinction can be made between an argument that is deductively valid (as outlined above) and inductively forceful. An argument is deductive if the conclusion is certain; it is inductive if the conclusion is likely or probable, but not certain. See Bowell and Kemp, *Critical Thinking*, pp. 64–100.

[3] This wording is taken from the 1984 edition of the NIV Bible. The 2011 translation reads as, 'Scripture cannot be set aside'.

[4] As Tom Wright puts it, 'It used to be said that the New Testament writers "didn't think they were writing Scripture". That is hard to sustain historically today. The fact that their writings were, in various senses, "occasional" ... is not to the point. At precisely those points of urgent need (when, for instance, writing Galatians or 2 Corinthians) Paul is

most conscious that he is writing as one authorized, by the apostolic call he has received from Jesus Christ, and in the power of the Spirit, to bring life and order to the church by his words.' N.T. Wright, *The Last Word: Beyond the Bible Wars to a New Understanding of the Authority of Scripture* (San Francisco: HarperCollins, 2005), p. 51.

[5] An interesting discussion of this can be seen in Edmund L. Gettier, 'Is Justified True Belief Knowledge?', Analysis 23 (1963), pp. 121–23. Available at http://www.ditext.com/gettier/gettier.html

[6] A similar argument can be seen in C.S. Lewis' essay 'What Are We to Make of Jesus Christ?' in *God in the Dock* (edited by Walter Hooper; Fount: London, 1971), pp. 79–85.

[7] There is some debate about John's account possibly being written a little later, but given the absence of any mention in John's gospel of the cataclysmic events of AD 70 (when the Romans destroyed the Jerusalem temple), I favour a date pre-AD 70—which means even John's gospel is still written within thirty-five years of Jesus' death.

[8] For accounts of Jesus' death see Matthew 27:45–54; Mark 15:33–39; Luke 23:44–49; and John 19:28–37.

[9] See Matthew 28:5–7; Mark 16:6; Luke 24:1–3; and John 20:1–7.

[10] See also John 20:11–18.

[11] See also Matthew 28:16 and John 20:19–29; 21:1.

[12] Tim Keller, *Reason for God* (New York: Dutton, 2008), p. 202.

5. A FEW WORKED EXAMPLES

[1] You can find these stories at http://www.telegraph.co.uk/news/health/news/10717566/Aborted-babies-incinerated-to-heat-UK-hospitals.html and http://www.theguardian.com/society/2015/jul/15/planned-parenthood-fetal-tissue-video-republican-reaction. Cited 6 August 2015.

[2] For an example of the former see the article on the *New Statesman* website by Sarah Ditum entitled 'My Body, My Choice': http://www.newstatesman.com/politics/2014/11/my-body-my-choice-now-abortion-rights-must-be-fought-first-principles. For an example of the latter see the quotes within the following brief piece on the *TIME* magazine website: http://time.com/3854543/abortion-debate/

[3] You can see some examples by running a Google search on 'idscforlife'.

[4] It should be said that modern palliative care is excellent and as such, in the majority of cases, a slow painful death is not inevitable.

[5] Since God exists outside of time and space he is able to perceive the totality of our existence from his eternal perspective.

[6] See https://yougov.co.uk/news/2013/05/20/voters-back-same-sex-marriage/

[7] See especially Romans 1:25–27.

CONCLUSION

[1] H.L. Mencken, 'The Divine Afflatus' in *A Mencken Chrestomathy* (New York: Vintage, 1982), p. 443.